Artifacts of Loss

Artifacts of Loss

Crafting Survival in Japanese American Concentration Camps

JANE E. DUSSELIER

RUTGERS UNIVERSITY PRESS

NEW BRUNSWICK, NEW JERSEY, AND LONDON

Library of Congress Cataloging-in-Publication Data

Dusselier, Jane E. (Jane Elizabeth)
    Artifacts of loss : crafting survival in Japanese American concentration camps /
Jane E. Dusselier.
        p. cm.
    Includes bibliographical references and index.
    ISBN 978–0–8135–4407–6 (hbk. : alk. paper)
    ISBN 978–0–8135–4408–3 (pbk. : alk. paper)
    1. Japanese Americans—Evacuation and relocation, 1942–1945—Psychological
aspects.   2. Concentration camps—United States—Psychological aspects.
3. Concentration camp inmates as artists—United States.   4. Japanese American
decorative arts.   5. Japanese Americans—Material culture.   I. Title.
    D769.8.A6D87 2008
    940.531773—dc22   2008007759

A British Cataloging-in-Publication record for this book is available from the British Library.

Visit our Web site: http://rutgerspress.rutgers.edu

Manufactured in the United States of America

To Barbara Judd, who sparked my interest in this topic, and Tobie Matava, whose support and love mean everything to me. And in remembrance of all those imprisoned in Japanese American concentration camps.

Contents

List of Illustrations   ix
Acknowledgments   xiii

1   Visual Accounts of Loss   1

2   Remaking Inside Places   14

3   Re-territorializing Outside Spaces   51

4   Making Connections   88

5   Mental Landscapes of Survival   125

6   Contemporary Legacies of Loss   154

Notes   167
Index   197

Illustrations

1   Living unit at Tanforan   15

2   Cabinet made by a Tule Lake crafter   23

3   Table and chairs made from found materials at Topaz   24

4   Embroidered landscapes served as colorful wall hangings at Heart Mountain   28

5   Carved clay tablet depicting the Heart Mountain landscape   28

6   Artificial flowers made at Manzanar   31

7   Artificial roses made at Manzanar   31

8   An example of ikebana from Jerome   33

9   Kobu was a popular art form in the Arkansas camps   37

10   A bon-kei and ikebana display at Amache   38

11   Nameplates helped internees distinguish their living unit from that of their neighbors at Amache   39

12   A nameplate made from woven cotton yarn at Amache   40

13   Wooden spoons made from discarded apple crates at Heart Mountain   44

14   Making furniture for schools at Heart Mountain   47

15   School furniture made by Manzanar internees   48

16   Intricately carved butsudans created by internees were used in camp-wide services   49

17   Internees quickly transformed the areas around their living quarters   54

18 Garden in front of a Tanforan barrack   56

19 Internees arriving at Topaz found a flat, dust-filled landscape   61

20 Manzanar barrack garden   64

21 Harvesting daikon at Gila River   66

22 The climate and soil conditions at Rohwer produced
    lush gardens   68

23 Preparing the soil for spring planting at Heart Mountain   70

24 Woman working in a Manzanar community garden   74

25 Potato planting at Tule Lake   77

26 Playing golf on Manzanar's dirt- and dust-filled fairways   79

27 Ice-skating was a popular winter activity at Heart Mountain   82

28 Walkways constructed at Rohwer helped internees avoid
    ankle-deep dust or muddy silt   85

29 Manzanar before and after   86

30 Camp-made outdoor play equipment at Tule Lake   91

31 Typical interior scene in one Manzanar barrack   95

32 Lapel pin made at Topaz   97

33 Picture of a dog drawn at Poston and mailed   100

34 Small items made with shells and wood were often given
    as gifts   101

35 Small objects were easily mailed to friends beyond the
    camp boundaries   103

36 Attending exhibits was a popular activity in most camps   104

37 Wood carvings made by students participating in the adult
    education classes at Amache   105

38 Kobu used as a vase   106

39 Kobu artists at Rohwer and Jerome frequently displayed
    their works   108

40 A wide range of art was exhibited at camp shows   112

41 Much needlework featured floral designs   114

42 Heart Mountain art class   117

43 Jewelry created from discarded tin cans at Rohwer   122

44 Some Japanese Americans were driven to suicide by their
    internment experience   128

45 Senninbari vests were made to protect friends, husbands,
    sons, and brothers who joined the U.S. armed forces   130

46 Masahiro's artwork was often mailed to his father, who was
    imprisoned in a Department of Justice facility   133

47 Funeral wreaths at Heart Mountain   136

48 Women making artificial flowers   137

49 Boys carving model planes at Poston   140

50 Girls proudly display the dolls they made at the
    Labor Day Festival   143

51 Father and son carve small wooden animals   147

52 Manzanar craftsman making getas   149

53 Bird lapel pins made from scrap wood   153

Acknowledgments

Artifacts of Loss owes much to many archivists, librarians, and community activists. I struck gold in Powell, Wyoming, both in terms of primary sources and a new friend, when I met Ladonna Zall, who serves on the board of the Heart Mountain Foundation, an organization committed to remembering the imprisonment of Japanese Americans. Zall is the organization's archivist and cares for a rich collection of artifacts. Jane Beckwith welcomed to me Delta, Utah, and the archival holdings of the Topaz Museum. She graciously and enthusiastically supported this project from my first phone call to her. Beth Porter was my archival host at the Eastern California Museum, providing encouragement as I worked my way through the museum's extensive collection of oral histories and artifacts. She is an incredibly competent archivist who knows her collection. When I arrived in McGehee, Arkansas, on a warm June afternoon, Rosalie Santine Gould treated me to a delicious poor-boy sandwich at the local golf club and then showed me her collection of Rohwer artifacts. She is devoted to gathering and preserving camp-made art and contributed to the successful efforts to designate Rohwer a national landmark. Johanna Lewis, a history professor at the University of Arkansas, Little Rock, helped me locate oral histories and artifacts related to the Rohwer and Jerome camps.

Many of the archives waived their fees, which has allowed me to include a powerful selection of photographs. Along with the aforementioned organizations, archives, and activists, the following archives granted me permission to publish their images free of charge, for which I thank them: the Department of Special Collections in the Charles E. Young Research Library at UCLA; the Hinckley Library at Northwest College in Powell, Wyoming; the Life Interrupted Papers at the University of Arkansas, Little Rock; and the Department of Special Collections at California State University, Sacramento.

I was lucky to have three supportive editors at Rutgers University Press. Melanie Halkias expressed interest in this project from the start. I first presented a paper on my work at an Association for Asian American Studies conference, where Gary Okihiro kindly chaired the panel and acted as commentator. Melanie attended the panel and urged me to expand the paper into a volume. Kendra Boileau and Leslie Mitchner guided this book through the press. I'm especially thankful to Leslie, who offered suggestions on how to improve the book and was committed to including a wide selection of images. Thank you to Roger Daniels for reading the manuscript. His suggestions made *Artifacts of Loss* a much better book. And thank you to Kathryn Gohl, who was a thorough and thoughtful copyeditor.

I also thank Edith Mitko and Haruko Moriyasu, who helped track down oral histories and art created at the Topaz camp. Although they are not archivists, they were generous with their time, energy, and support. And finally, I thank Nancy Struna, Kandice Chuh, Jo Paoletti, and especially Robyn Muncy and the director of my dissertation, Seung-kyung Kim, whose belief in this project never failed.

Artifacts of Loss

CHAPTER 1

Visual Accounts of Loss

Testifying before the Commission on Wartime Relocation and Internment of Civilians on August 4, 1981, U.S. senator Sam Hayakawa described life in World War II Japanese American concentrations camps as "trouble-free and relatively happy."[1] Established by the U.S. Congress, the commission had been charged with examining the application of Executive Order 9066, signed by Franklin D. Roosevelt on February 19, 1942, and recommending "appropriate remedies."[2] Hayakawa's cheery characterization of camp life was immediately met with audible jeers from an audience of former internees and their descendants, to whom the Republican senator from California responded by asking: "How else can one account for the tremendous output of these amateur artists who, having time on their hands, turned out little masterpieces of sculpture, ceramics, painting, and flower arrangement?"[3] *Artifacts of Loss* takes up this question, but argues that camp-made art, broadly defined, aided internees in repositioning themselves in hostile environments. By creating art, imprisoned Japanese Americans attained visibilities and voices that incorporated heterogeneity and challenged exploitive racialization.

Rather than understanding camp-made art as evidence of humane treatment, I suggest that these material cultures comprised diverse visual accounts of loss, and physical as well as mental landscapes of survival. This thesis offers two parallel yet distinguishable forms of analysis, one perhaps belonging more to the past and the other to the present. The historical consideration addresses my interpretation of the meanings and purposes of camp-made art for imprisoned Japanese Americans. *Artifacts* offers four such meanings, which are explored in individual chapters. In chapter 2, "Remaking Inside Places," I discuss how internees employed art to rework their physical locations of imprisonment into places of survival. Both at temporary imprisonment facilities and later at permanent concentration camps, internees were confronted with filthy and deplorable living quarters. Many of the temporary living units, located on the grounds of racetracks, were formerly horse stalls. Even at permanent sites of confinement, dwelling units were crudely constructed barracks with abundant and gaping cracks that provided easy entry for sand, dirt, and cold.

These inside places were modified by internees as they responded to degraded living conditions by creating furniture from discarded apple crates, cardboard, tree branches and stumps, scrap pieces of wood left behind by government carpenters, and wood lifted from guarded lumber piles. Having addressed their needs for beds, chairs, and tables, internees turned their attention to aesthetic matters by creating needlework, wood carvings, ikebana, paintings, shell art, and kobu. Living quarters evolved into more bearable places made meaningful by camp-made and displayed art that created visual dialogues at least partially controlled by internees. Through and with art, many imprisoned Japanese Americans spoke of their commitment to survival as they improved the materiality of their lives by altering dwellings spaces. In this way, art helped internees to reposition themselves in hostile settings.

Dramatic changes to outside spaces were also critical for altering external spaces of confinement into survivable landscapes. In chapter 3, "Re-territorializing Outside Spaces," I examine changes made to the landscapes of both temporary imprisonment facilities and concentration camps. Camp geographies were re-territorialized when internees created vegetable and flower gardens, pebbled walkways, and elaborate landscaping projects. In this context, re-territorialization is the process by which hostile and unfamiliar spaces are modified into arenas where identities can be articulated and marginalized people can declare differences and enact subjectivities.[4] America's concentration camps were spatial expressions of race based on the U.S. government's concentration of Japanese Americans in geographically specific locations. But internees worked to alter these physical landscapes of confinement by joining aesthetics and politics through the art forms of gardening and landscaping. Vegetable, fruit, and rock gardens, as well as skating rinks, golf courses, and swimming pools, were, in the words of Akhil Gupta and James Ferguson, "conceptual and political acts of re-imagination" on the part of internees.[5] By inscribing camp landscapes with these art forms, internees imagined and enacted portable senses of place.

In chapter 4, "Making Connections," I position art as a means of making connections, a framework that helps us escape utopian thinking and models of community building that overemphasize the development of common beliefs, ideas, and practices that supposedly unify people into identifiable groups.[6] Creating art sustained, reformed, and created new relationships among family members and friends. By sewing clothes for each other, presenting gifts of artificial flowers and lapel pins, and participating in classes and exhibits, internees addressed their needs for maintaining and developing relationships. From this perspective, camp-made art helps us understand how internees connected with one another in the context of heterogeneity that encompassed a range of differences, including those of sex, generation, date of immigration, class, religion, language, age, and occupation. This idea of making connections takes on more meaning when we remember that these new prisoners of the U.S. government experienced a series of displacements as they were forcibly removed from their homes and then incarcerated in temporary imprisonment facilities, only to be later moved to more distant, permanent concentration camps. Art provided internees with mediums through which they were able to create connections among themselves on the basis of identifying with each other rather than being identical to one another. In this way, art created and sustained a myriad of intricate and layered connections. "Making Connections" addresses how art helped internees connect with one another in the context of heterogeneity and almost limitless differences.

In chapter 5, "Mental Landscapes of Survival," I explore how some internees linked the creation of art with their own emotional and mental well-being. Creating, exhibiting, consuming, living with, and thinking about art became embedded in the everyday patterns of camp life for many internees and helped provide a context for mental, emotional, and psychic survival. Even in the bleakest of conditions, art aided imprisoned Japanese Americans in creating strategies to improve the psychic conditions of their lives and fashion mental spaces of survival. Here they attempted to join individual and personal visions with collective considerations by making and exhibiting their art. Many nonartists participated in this process by consuming camp-made art. Camp artists reached beyond aesthetic considerations, employing art as a method to ensure emotional subsistence in psychically and materially oppressive environments. Art materialized the psychic lives of internees, helping them link individual concerns with social life. In chapter 5, I ask readers to think about art and everyday objects as critical to mental and emotional health.

Although my analysis of the meanings of camp-made art may be more easily understood in context of the past, I intend my concluding chapter to resonate more deeply with the present. In chapter 6, "Contemporary Legacies of Loss," I argue that past losses of imprisoned Japanese Americans are applicable to the present. By creating art in forms such as flowers made with tissue paper, wood carvings of pets left behind, and furniture from discarded apple crates, internees revealed and asserted their many losses. Considering what "was lost in terms of what remains," this chapter positions camp-made art as creating narratives that bring past losses and, by association, past oppressions into the present moment. From this perspective, losses such as those produced by Executive Order 9066 encompass half-lives with which we must continue to engage in the present. While imprisoned, Japanese American women, children, and men employed art to remake the physical landscapes of the camps into livable places, establish new and reform existing connections, and create mental spaces of survival. They also generated lasting legacies for those of us interested in social justice. In the last chapter, I join with recent scholars pointing to the intellectual, cultural, and political meanings of loss.[7]

Using these ideas of loss, I hope to further expand artifactual evidence beyond the realm of museums, which often construct unified, national narratives based on consensus. Art like that created in Japanese American concentrations camps is best situated in political arenas where differences are valued and objects understood as provoking human responses that lead to change. Employing the ideas of loss to study art created by imprisoned Japanese Americans will help us as we emphasize transnational understandings of culture and identity and frame our scholarship in contexts of globalization. By studying a wide range of camp-made art, we learn that place, even when it is denied by the power of nation-states, can reside in portable spaces such as art. This book addresses global movements of people by attempting to understand how Japanese Americans who experienced a series of voluntary, coerced, and forced displacements recuperated a sense of place.

Some readers may be hesitant to think of the everyday objects I discuss as art, but most of these camp-made crafts adhere to *Cambridge Dictionary*'s definition of art as "the making of objects, images, music, etc. that are beautiful or that express feelings."[8] Many internees shared interests and time, creating a wide range of what some readers may describe as crafts, folk art, material culture, or hobbies. Among these objects were finger rings created with peach pits and toothbrush handles, furniture constructed from discarded orange crates, hats created with grasses gathered on camp grounds, flowers made from Kleenex tissues and crepe paper, jewelry made from shells, canes carved from ironwood, and dresses sewn from discarded rice bags. The labels we give these objects are laden with cultural meaning and power, especially when we consider the art of Asian Americans within the conventional Eurocentric cannon. With this in mind, I use the terms *art*, *craft*, and *material culture* interchangeably to include all forms of cultural expression that result in a physical object. My use of these terms is intended to disturb a hierarchy of cultural expressions in which objects classified as art are imbued with more legitimacy, meaning, and significance. This interpretation asks readers to expand their definition of art to include objects created by people with little or no formal training and who use a wide range of materials and diverse skills.

This volume complements an established body of work concerned with concentration camp art. Rather than studying the activities of everyday crafters, however, previous scholarship about concentration camp art focused on the work of professionally trained artists who expressed their creativity through "fine art," including watercolors, oils, woodblock prints, and sketches. Outstanding examples of this burgeoning area of study include Kimi Kodani Hill's monograph exploring the life of her grandfather Chiura Obata, Kristine Kim's work on Henry Sugimoto, Karin Higa's exhibition catalogue, *The View from Within: Japanese American Art from the Internment Camps, 1942–1945*, and Deborah Gesensway and Mindy Roseman's *Beyond Words: Images from America's Concentration Camps*.[9] Although the works of prominent painters have captured the interests of internment scholars, more common forms of cultural and artistic expression have remained outside the realm of scholarly inquiry.

Artifacts addresses this gap, concentrating on everyday art forms created by imprisoned Japanese Americans with little or no formal artistic training. Only two books have been published on the topic of crafting activities in the camps, which is surprising considering the volume of art created. A highly illustrated volume titled *Beauty behind Barbed Wire* (1952) contains photographs of crafts, but the author is more intent on congratulating the War Relocation Authority for "one of the finest achievements in American war and peacetime government administration" than revealing the lives of camp crafters or the meanings of their work. A portfolio-sized photographic book titled *The Art of Gaman* (2005) emphasizes the striking aesthetics of the objects over their political meanings.[10] Recognizing this void, *Artifacts* focuses on the political consequences and uses of camp-made material culture.

Although strongly disagreeing with Senator Hayakawa's positive portrayal of camp-made art, previous explorations of this topic have treated concentration camp art as less than radical, instead attributing high levels of artistic production to an increase in leisure time available to internees.[11] This reading of crafting activities has come to be known as the "forced leisure" interpretation. Because they are more canonized and privileged, the works of professionally trained artists skirt the forced leisure interpretation because they adhere to accepted aesthetic standards while also serving a documentary function. These artists were not simply whiling away their time but creating "true" or legitimate pieces of art that provided literal and much-needed records of internment experiences. A forced leisure interpretation of camp-made art is problematic because it suggests that internee artwork is evidence of humane treatment.

Rather than focusing our attention on the harsh conditions and struggles for survival, the forced leisure interpretation encourages us to see images of internees with an abundance of free time on their hands, occupying themselves with carving, sewing, and planting gardens. This interpretation belies the recorded experiences of many imprisoned Japanese Americans, who worked as camp cooks, doctors, nurses, teachers, and boiler tenders to keep conditions in the camps livable, while also struggling with basic survival. Because living units lacked plumbing, internees spent much of their time in long lines waiting to eat and attend to personal hygiene. Along with being poorly designed and constructed, communal latrines, bathing spaces, and laundry facilities were too few in number to adequately accommodate camp populations. In this context, it becomes more apparent that the motivation of internees involved in crafting activities was not simply to fill leisure time and prevent boredom. While the free time of internees certainly varied, evidence suggests that many found time in their busy schedules to participate in crafting activities.[12]

Many students of the internment argue that high levels of artistic expression among imprisoned Japanese Americans should not surprise us. Indeed, some interpret the creation of art by internees as representing a "thrilling revelation of fine innate culture."[13] Elaine Kim argues that Asian artistic expression has been viewed as "a harmless racial and cultural trait passed down as if in the genes."[14] From Kim's perspective, Asian American artistic abilities serve as markers of racial difference and are problematically grounded in an ancient, unchanging, and singular Asian culture. Representing this mythical Asianness and undergoing a process of orientalization, the artistic successes of Asian Americans are understood as nonthreatening because the products are interpreted as exotic, feminine, and extraneous. From this perspective, high levels of art making in Japanese American concentration camps were, and unfortunately continue to be, understood as natural, predictable, and harmless expressions of Asian culture, requiring no explanation or analysis.

A review of crafting literature, however, provides convincing evidence that prolific artists and crafters exist among most groups of people, especially those experiencing marginalization. During the first thirty years of the twentieth century, itinerant carvers in the United States often exchanged small intricate boxes made from pieces of scrap wood for a meal or a night's rest in a warm, clean bed. These "tramp artists" also produced a wider range of objects for selling or gift giving, including furniture, elaborate picture frames, tea sets, and wall clocks.[15] Art created by African Americans during the last third of the twentieth century was the subject of a massive two-volume work titled *Souls Grown Deep: African American Vernacular Art of the South*. With little formal education, these "vernacular artists" from eleven southern states employed a wide range of found and discarded materials to produce diverse art forms. Among the objects created were paintings, sculptures, carvings, and yard art made with tree roots, chewing gum, buttons, house paint, cinder blocks, chunks of concrete, rocks, tree branches, tin cans, and nails. Rather than purchasing expensive brushes, paints, and canvas, ninety-year-old Jimmie Lee Sudduth created paintings by dipping his fingers in stains made from berries, grass, and mud and then drawing on scraps of wood and iron. As Sudduth reported: "I got twenty-three colors of mud in my own yard."[16] Similar to the creations of imprisoned Japanese Americans, those of itinerant carvers and African American vernacular artists were made of scrap lumber, discarded fruit crates, tree roots, rocks, and other found materials. All three groups of artists created material cultures that spoke of their experiences and visions for the future.

Quilts and other forms of patchwork are well-known examples of crafting among diverse groups of people, ranging from seventeenth-century settlers arriving on the eastern seaboard to slaves escaping on the Underground Railroad. For centuries, Appalachian artists living in the poorest region of the United States created quilts using scraps of calico, muslin dyed with indigo, and with animal-feed bags for batting.[17] We can also look at the resistive importance of quilt making for African American slaves. Jacqueline L. Tobin and Raymond G. Dobard argue that slaves devised a complex system of oral and visual communication by making and studying quilts.[18] Designs and patterns functioned as codes in a complex language that instructed slaves preparing for their escape, improved the likelihood of their survival during the journey, and provided directions for them while traveling on the Underground Railroad. Stitching was an integral part of this language, with the length and position of threads relaying specific meanings. Once these "visual maps of freedom" were "mastered" and the time of escape drew near, quilts were placed on fences to serve as mnemonic devices and instruct slaves to take specific actions.

As this literature shows, crafting is not a "natural" activity linked to racial identities but is employed by diverse groups of people to form identities and ensure survival. Rather than connected to some imagined racial essentialism, the meanings of this art are contingent on the specificities of cultural, historical, political, economic, and geographical contexts. Recognizing that crafting is a common experience for many Americans is not an argument for universalism but suggests that art is one aspect of culture that some people draw upon to survive. Although some forms of Japanese American concentration camp art encompassed cultural continuity, this observation should not lead us to the conclusion that Japanese Americans were more or less artistically inclined than any other cultural or racial group. We should also remember that art was only one cultural practice that internees relied on to create identifications with one another. Among other identifying activities were board and card games, sporting events, gambling, performing arts, work, cooking, reading and language clubs, and drinking.

For readers unfamiliar with the mass incarceration of all West Coast Japanese Americans during the period of World War II, some historical background may help place this art in context. As result of Executive Order 9066, signed on February 19, 1942, by President Franklin D. Roosevelt, more than 120,000 persons of Japanese ancestry living in the United States were forcibly removed from their homes and imprisoned in concentration camps. Most were U.S. citizens who had been affected in many ways by the century-long legacy of anti-Japanese discrimination that prevented first-generation Issei from becoming citizens of the United States or own- ing land and severely restricted the educational, employment, and housing opportunities of second-generation Nisei. A series of immigration acts passed by the U.S. Congress throughout the nineteenth century ensured that racism was supported by structures of the nation-state. Using hysteria generated by Pearl Harbor to justify this mass and illegal incarceration of Japanese Americans, the U.S. government ignored the unconstitutionality of imprisoning persons without charging them with crimes. With rulings from the Supreme Court, the federal government used race as the basis on which to incarcerate 120,000 innocent women, children, and men.

Japanese Americans were first confined in what the government euphemistically referred to as "assembly centers." Thirteen of these facilities were located in California and one each in Oregon, Arizona, and Washington, for a total of sixteen in all. Tulare, one of the temporary imprisonment facilities located in California, was the first to open on April 20, 1942. Housing a total of 5,061 Japanese Americans who previously resided in Los Angeles and Sacramento, Tulare reached its one-day peak of 4,978 on August 11. Fresno, also located in California at the Fresno County Fairgrounds, was the final confinement center to close after reaching a peak population of 5,120. On October 30, 1942, the last group of Japanese Americans were loaded onto trains and shipped to one of ten concentration camps.[19] By late October, 120,000 Japanese Americans were shipped to distant and desolate places of confinement, including Manzanar and Tule Lake (Newell) in California, Minidoka (Hunt) in Idaho, Jerome (Denson) and Rohwer in Arkansas, Heart Mountain in Wyoming, Granada (Amache) in Colorado, Poston (Colorado River) and Gila (Rivers) in Arizona, and Topaz in Utah.

Conditions in these camps were deplorable and filled with hardship. Simple yet necessary activities such as eating and bathing absorbed tremendous amounts of time and energy, and filled the days of many. Internees were required to stand in long mess-hall lines three times each day, in frigid winter conditions that sometimes caused frost bite and extreme summer temperatures that resulted in heat stroke. Time-consuming trips to communal outhouses and laundry facilities were also daily experiences. When we consider the lives of mothers, we gain a glimpse of the miseries endured. Because living quarters lacked running water, young mothers focused much of their time and energy on toting youngsters to and from communal latrines and bathing facilities, along with daily laundry trips.[20] Young mothers with infants fought the unending battle of keeping up with soiled diapers.

Cramped living conditions made the immediacy of washing freshly soiled diapers clear to all internees, even those with bad sniffers. Dirty

laundry required the constant attention and labor of women, otherwise
the smellscapes of living quarters became unbearable. A twenty-six-year-
old Nisei man imprisoned at Tanforan astutely observed: "The mothers
work as hard as ever with the exception of cooking. The laundry work
is probably much harder."[21] Keeping clothes clean was made even more
taxing by the flourlike dust that frequently soiled those freshly laun-
dered garments left hanging on outside lines to dry. One young woman
remembered that besides combating the lethargy caused by frequent and
nagging illnesses such as stomach upsets and colds, much of her energy
was consumed by "keeping our room dusted, swept, and mopped to be
rid of the constant accumulation of dust, and in trying to do laundry
when the water was running."[22]

Young children's unaccompanied trips to the latrine encompassed
tragic possibilities, as in the case of a boy imprisoned at Salinas who
slipped through a toilet seat made to army specifications for grown
men. Responding to screams coming from inside the privy, a passerby
found the youngster "in the hole hanging by his elbows" and rescued
him from a twenty-foot drop into human waste.[23] Internees at Poston's
Camp II were on alert for children in distress after several boys slipped
through the seats, got stuck, and required help to remove themselves.[24]
At Amache, rattlesnakes coiled in the dark, cool environs of outhouses,
posing yet another threat to carefree youngsters and forcing mothers
equipped with two-by-fours to make hourly sweeps before allowing even
older children to enter communal latrines.[25] Toilet training children in
these conditions was especially difficult and traumatic, leaving concerned mothers with few options but to provide emotional and physical
support and hope for the best.

Rooted in these material conditions of imprisonment, *Artifacts of
Loss* asks readers to think differently about identity, subjectivity, and
art with the hope of prompting a reconsideration of everyday objects
as critical to physical, mental, and emotional survival. Concentration
camp art activities, defined in the broadest terms, were not frivolous

but encompassed political possibilities. Beyond the histories of Japanese Americans, this project speaks to how oppression is lived and the place of art in the lives of marginalized people. Challenging the idea that subjectivity is always grounded in or a product of embodied identities, I offer art as a means by which people identify with each other and change their circumstances. In this volume, I expand our understandings of identity formation by advancing the idea that embodied sameness and identities may serve more powerfully as structures of oppression rather than templates of resistance. When we pay close attention to connections between art and the everyday materiality of life in Japanese American concentration camps, sameness based on embodied identity appears less important than differences created by thinking with and producing art. Through and with art, internees generated ideas, strategies, and visions for re-placing themselves in the context of larger and often hostile places and groups of people.

CHAPTER 2

Remaking Inside Places

By joining the need to create places of survival with practices of making art, many imprisoned Japanese Americans recuperated a portable sense of place. Some internees looked to the materiality of their lives to produce liberative practices. Hopes for generating even very limited degrees of comfort through the creation of art helped many camp crafters to improve the material conditions of their lives. By reworking inside places, internees spoke to each other through visual narratives that expressed emotions and commitments to survival. With art, internees generated new ideas that allowed the traumas of internment to be thought through.[1] This process of *re*-placing themselves in hostile landscapes began slowly, as internees altered the inside places of imprisonment locations. After long, tiring bus and train trips, the newly arrived internees often walked into small rooms usually measuring sixteen by twenty feet and furnished with a single light bulb hanging from the ceiling. In many cases, potbellied stoves, the only sources of heat, had not yet been installed. Internees were responsible for making their own mattresses by stuffing canvas and burlap sacks with straw. Of all the indignities encompassed by internment, a nineteen-year-old young woman found nighttimes filled with hay pricking her skin especially demeaning.[2]

Living quarters at temporary imprisonment facilities were constructed with little thought for the comfort, health, or dignity of the inhabitants.

1. Living unit at Tanforan, June 16, 1942. Photographer: Dorothea Lange.
Courtesy of the National Archives and Records Administration.

A father, mother, son, and two daughters, newly designated by the U.S.
government as family 10710, arrived at Puyallup, Washington, on April 28,
1942, and were assigned to unit 2–1-A, a single room measuring eighteen
by twenty feet. Located thirty-five miles south of Seattle at the Western
Washington State Fairgrounds, the new "home" of the Itoi family was
bare except for a small wood-burning stove. A recently constructed floor
of unseasoned two-by-fours rested directly on the ground . A bumper crop
of dandelions was pushing up through the numerous and ample cracks
between the floorboards, evidence of hurried and faulty construction.[3]

Conditions were even more crowded for a widowed mother and her seven children who were forcibly removed from their home in Colusa, California, and confined in a fourteen-by-fourteen living unit located on the Merced County Fairgrounds. To make matters worse, Merced's living units were separated by thin partitions reaching only halfway to the ceiling, an environment in which privacy was impossible for this family of eight, with all seven children under the age of eighteen.[4] A pregnant woman imprisoned at Fresno found survival particularly difficult. Summer temperatures reaching over 110 degrees and a smells-cape permeated with horse manure provoked extreme measures from a nauseated and weakened Violet De Cristoforo. First she wrapped herself in a wet towel and crawled under a bed, but when this failed to relieve her symptoms, De Cristoforo dug a hole and took shelter in the cooler environs of the earth.[5]

At Tanforan Racetrack, in San Bruno, California, Tsuyako Kitashima, her mother, and three brothers were assigned to a small horse stall but spent most of their time outside in their efforts to avoid the stench of manure.[6] Thankful for even meager improvements, another family imprisoned at Tanforan was moved from their horse stall to newly constructed barracks in July, after enduring temperatures reaching over one hundred degrees. Although it was "rough," the new living unit included a window, which made hot afternoons more bearable. But now family members found themselves battling excessively dusty conditions, which caused persistent respiratory ailments including sore throats, colds, and asthma.[7] Also shipped by bus to Tanforan, Yoshiko Uchida's family was assigned to barrack 16, a long barn previously used to stable race horses. Arriving at stall 40, the family of four looked into a filthy room measuring ten by twenty feet, with three folded army cots leaning against a wall. Floorboards saturated with horse manure had been hastily covered with linoleum, producing an especially sickening odor.

Living conditions at Topaz, in Utah, the Uchidas' final place of imprisonment, remained harsh and difficult. Having endured two exhausting nights on dirty and dilapidated trains, many internees shipped from Tanforan to the desert town of Delta, Utah, arrived in a weakened state and suffering from severe motion sickness.[8] Most of the trains transporting internees from temporary to permanent imprisonment facilities had been retrieved from storage after being retired. They were fitted with nonfunctioning gas light fixtures and contained hard, straight-back seats that made sleeping impossible. The Uchidas, after their train ride, boarded a bus for the remaining seventeen-mile drive to Topaz. Upon arrival, they were assigned to a dusty twenty-by-eighteen-foot room identified as block 7, barrack 3, unit 3. Empty except for army cots, the walls of this room were distinguished by enormous and abundant cracks that allowed dirt from frequent dust storms unfettered access to every inch of living space.[9] Some Topaz internees responded to these conditions by pulling up the floorboards, digging ten feet into the earth, and creating basements that were warm in the winter, cool in the summer, and relatively free of dust.[10] Degraded living conditions and shoddy concentration camp construction are memorialized even today by the term "Topaz carpenter," a derogatory expression used by contemporary residents of Millard County, Utah, when referring to construction workers who produce poorly built and substandard structures.[11]

For internees being transferred from Pomona, California, to Heart Mountain, Wyoming, conditions were more severe in that these train passengers were forced to endure four long sleepless nights. Because the train had attracted rock-throwing mobs on previous trips, anxious armed guards, hoping to hide the identity of their passengers, insisted that window shades be drawn throughout the entire journey. Exhausted internees walked into drafty, cold living units furnished with a coal stove and metal army cots.[12] Bedding was a persistent problem, with internees perplexed about where and how to sleep. Many newly arrived Japanese Americans created "mattresses" by stuffing burlap sacks with straw, although while stuffing they had to be on the lookout to avoid snakes and scorpions. When mattress-making supplies and blankets ran low, some internees doubled up and shared a single cot, padding the wire springs with one blanket and attempting to stay warm under the other. Fusaye Hashimoto remembered surviving her first cold nights at Manzanar, in California, by sharing a blanket and cot with her sister.[13]

Although cold temperatures confronted Japanese Americans confined at Heart Mountain and Manzanar, heat was a formidable problem for internees arriving by bus at Poston, in Arizona. A twenty-seven-year-old Nisei man from Fountain Valley, California, described his Camp I living quarters in three words: "It was hot!" Worried about the climate, he remembered that his first impression was that "a lot of guys were going to die."[14] Even mainstream media sources commented on the degrading living conditions, with a *Catholic Digest* article best summing up the impression of reporters visiting the Granada camp at Amache, Colorado. "No one has starved, and no one has frozen; but this is about as much as can be said in defense of the centers as housing projects."[15] These temperature extremes were especially traumatic for people accustomed to the moderate West Coast climates of California and Washington.

Furniture making was the most immediate art activity of many internees during the first days of imprisonment, as they attempted to transform the shoddily built and dilapidated barracks into adequate shelter.[16] Often, furniture building occurred twice: first at the temporary imprisonment facilities, euphemistically referred to by the government as "assembly centers," and then again at one of the ten permanent concentration camps such as Topaz (Utah), Heart Mountain (Wyoming), and Gila (Arizona). Even though Japanese Americans recognized that their confinement in "assembly centers" would be short-lived, they immediately began employing art in the form of furniture making to create places of survival. Men were the most active participants in this art form, with wood understood as a manly medium, but some women crossed these gendered crafting lines to help furnish living units with camp-made tables, chairs, beds, shelves, desks, benches, partitions, and closets.[17] In an article assuring readers that "women can be carpenters too," a camp newspaper reported on the chairs, shelves, and tables created by Mrs. Toba in 4–23.[18]

Following the example of other internees, a father of two young daughters used his first day at the temporary imprisonment site in Puyallup, Washington, to scavenge the grounds for lumber and nails left by the contractors responsible for building the camp.[19] By the end of the first month, his new creations included a writing table, benches, shelves, and sliding wooden storage platforms that fit discreetly beneath each cot. Perhaps the most prized piece of camp-made furniture was a specially designed wooden cabinet that concealed the family's "illegal" hot plate from armed guards conducting surprise searches for "contraband."[20] Hot plates were especially valued possessions, with many internees ignoring regulations prohibiting cooking in the living units, where they prepared infant formula and other foods on these small electric devices.[21] Although they risked blowing the fuses and plunging an entire barrack into darkness, many internees willingly exchanged evenings without power for the satisfaction of "home"-cooked meals prepared on hotplates.

A woman from Los Angeles remembered that when, as a sixteen-year-old, she was imprisoned at Santa Anita, her family made their room "as livable as possible" with camp-made curtains and furnishings.[22] A racetrack prior to March 27, 1942, when the first Japanese Americans arrived, Santa Anita eventually contained nearly 19,000 internees, with many living in stables that formerly housed race horses.[23] Upon arrival at Puyallup, another teenager immediately began searching the barbwire-fenced area for scrap lumber left behind when the camp was being constructed. Hoping to provide his family with a minimum level of "comfort," William Kimura used these scavenged materials to build furniture.[24] A Hayward, California, teenager experienced feelings of despair during her first weeks of imprisonment at Stockton, but followed the example of her parents and pitched in to help "beautify their apartment." Although these physical improvements did not remedy the emotional anguish and physical discomforts caused by the implementation of Executive Order 9066, they did aid Nobuko Hanzawa in resituating herself in a hostile environment and better ensured her mental and physical survival. Remaking the physical environment of her living unit was critical to "pulling through the mist of confusion" for this youngster, who had been forcibly removed from her home in a rural area just south of San Francisco.[25]

Many furniture-making efforts were the result of lengthy trial and error, as was the case at Tanforan when shelves built by Florence Miho Nakamura's father gave way in the middle of the night, creating a racket heard throughout the barrack. Although housed in one of the newly constructed barracks rather than in a former horse stall, the Nakamura family lived in one of the units separated by thin walls reaching only halfway to the ceiling. As evidenced by the startled responses of Naka-mura's new neighbors to the collapsing shelves, noise traveled easily from unit to unit, and the thin walls provided little privacy.[26] Also pointing to the thinness of walls was a warning in Tanforan's newspaper about the dangers of "involuntary inoculations" caused by internees standing too close to walls while next-door neighbors were hanging newly completed shelves and cabinets. As the *Tanforan Totalizer* reported, one internee narrowly escaped being nailed in the back as the "energetic party in the next stall" hung a shelf on the wall.[27]

After using art to create minimal levels of comfort at the temporary imprisonment facilities, most internees were forced to pack up their few possessions and board trains for more distant and desolate locations.[28] Charles Kikuchi remembered looking around the room that had constituted his family's living quarters during their two and a half months of imprisonment at Tanforan and recalled how much their "home" had changed since their arrival on April 30, 1942. The Kikuchis had taken down a stable door and hung camp-made curtains to partition the room in which the family lived. Along with the curtains, the family furnishings now included camp-made benches, chairs, two wardrobes, a bureau, art objects that rested on shelves, and a desk built at the foot of his younger brother Jack's bed. In preparation for their transfer to Gila, Arizona, the Kikuchi family worked together throughout the morning of August 29 to carefully dismantle and pack their Tanforan furniture, "nails and all." Friends already shipped off to permanent concentration camps had written to inform the family of serious wood shortages, so, as Charles wrote in his diary, "any piece of lumber that we have is going with us."[29] Before boarding trains for transport to Topaz, another Tanforan internee converted his family's camp-made furniture into packing crates, which in turn were transformed back into tables, shelves, and benches upon arrival in the Utah desert.[30]

At their permanent locations of incarceration, internees again set to creating habitable places of survival by making furniture. After four long days on a train destined for Rohwer, Arkansas, Yoshio Matsuda stepped onto Arkansas soil with the goal of gathering wood to make a bed.[31] A teenage girl recently transferred from Santa Anita to Poston, Arizona, reported in a letter written to a librarian friend back home in California that many internees were becoming skilled at making beds from scrap lumber. After several nights attempting to sleep in a sagging army cot provided by the War Relocation Authority, she better understood the motivation of these crafters, observing: "The cot sinks down in the middle while the wooden bed stays straight."[32] Some new arrivals at Granada, in Amache, Colorado, immediately began constructing beds from scavenged wood, but supplies were soon exhausted, and many spent their first restless nights on straw-covered floors.[33] Seven hundred and fifty miles to the west in Topaz, Utah, a young girl felt less anxious sleeping in a bunk bed constructed by her father.[34]

Having devised adequate sleeping spaces, crafters shifted their attention to other types of furniture, including privacy screens, night stands, shelves, chests, chairs, and tables.[35] Describing her family's living unit at Amache, Colorado, as "nothing but a big room," Yoshie Mary Tashima had her spirits lifted by the furniture made by her brothers from scrap lumber.[36] Two brothers imprisoned at Topaz, Utah, transformed the

wooden crate that once protected their new potbellied stove into a
five-foot-long cushionless couch.[37] Countering the gendered image of
furniture makers with the headline "She Makes 'Em Herself," the *Manzanar Free Press* reported that Fumi Marumoto of block 9 created a small
bench and a "closet of shelves" from a discarded orange crate and cardboard boxes.[38] As a Minidoka internee remembered, the idea of comfort
remained uppermost in the minds of Japanese Americans as they again
repositioned themselves in harsh places of imprisonment by creating
furniture from found materials.[39]

Desperately needing privacy, internees constructed screens and
partitions from scrap wood, spare blankets, and cloth. Some internees
extended walls of individual living units to the ceiling, whereas others
partitioned their already small rooms into sleeping and living areas.[40]
While attending an art exhibit at Tulare, an Issei woman admired a
privacy screen, noting in a diary entry that the item had been made
by meticulously piecing together small pieces of scrap wood.[41] At Tule
Lake, California, administration officials reacted negatively to repeated
requests from internees for partition-making supplies. But when new
barracks were constructed to house supposed troublemakers from other
concentration camps, the men, women, and children already imprisoned
at Tule Lake lost little time taking advantage of the fresh supply piles in
the camp lumberyard. As one internee reported, "our luck changed" and
"we band[ed] together to attack in groups."[42] One youngster imprisoned
at Tule Lake recalled that these camp-made screens made her family's
"barren room look a bit more homey."[43]

Many women and children who endured imprisonment without their
husbands and fathers accepted the help of neighbors who offered to make
furniture.[44] With her husband imprisoned in the Department of Justice
facility at Lordsburg, New Mexico, Yukiko Furata and her four daughters
eagerly accepted a gift of camp-made tables to furnish their living unit
at Poston.[45] In a separate yet parallel incarceration, Furata's husband
was among thousands of Issei rounded up by the FBI in the aftermath

2. Cabinet made by a Tule Lake crafter, July 1, 1942. Photographer: Francis Stewart. Courtesy of the National Archives and Records Administration.

of Pearl Harbor and held in Department of Justice facilities. In a similar case, Dwight Takashi Uchida was arrested before nightfall on December 7 and imprisoned in the Department of Justice facility at Missoula, Montana. Nearly five months later, Uchida's wife and two daughters were forced from their Berkeley home and transported, under armed guard,

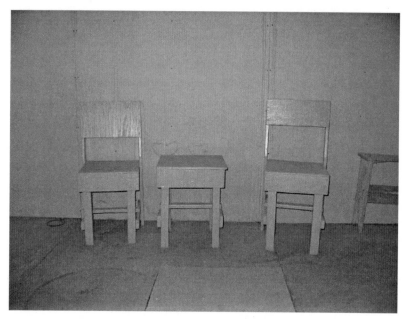

3. Table and chairs made from found materials at Topaz. Courtesy of the
Topaz Museum.

to Tanforan and later Topaz, Utah. Thankful to be imprisoned alongside
old friends, the female Uchidas relied on neighbors to build shelves, a
table, and two benches.[46] Revealing the total lack of reason underpin-
ning internment of the over 120,000 Japanese Americans was the case
of a woman imprisoned without her husband because he was ordered to
train Navy intelligence officers in Boulder, Colorado. Shipped to Amache,
Colorado, from Santa Anita during September 1942, this wife and mother
was too busy caring for two young sons to be concerned with building
furniture. Fortunately, neighbors quickly recognized her predicament
as a single mother and presented her with small chairs and tables pieced
together from scrap wood.[47] In the case of a widowed mother and two
daughters imprisoned first at Stockton and later at Rohwer, the eldest
daughter enlisted the help of three male friends, who transformed one-
by-twelve-inch pieces of lumber into shelves and benches.[48]

Supplies for making furniture were difficult to come by and proved to be the most significant obstacle for furniture makers. Careful to avoid the attention of armed soldiers in guard towers, internees restricted their early searches for furniture-building materials to well within the barbed-wire perimeters. Furniture makers dug and sifted through soil surrounding newly constructed barracks for discarded nails, while others hiked throughout the camps looking for scraps of lumber, discarded fruit crates, and cardboard boxes.[49] At Poston, furniture makers scoured the camp grounds for ironwood, mesquite, and sagebrush roots.[50] Persistent and enduring shortages of furniture-making supplies prompted many internees, primarily men, to take War Relocation Authority carpentry jobs. By securing these positions, camp carpenters established easier access to nails and wood for building chairs, benches, tables, and other "knickknacks" that made living units more habitable.[51] Understanding nails as prized possessions is likely difficult for many readers, but for imprisoned Japanese Americans, furniture-building materials were considered extraordinarily generous gifts. A woman imprisoned at Gila, Arizona, remembered giving nails, many of them bent, as an engagement gift to her friend. Gathered by sifting through sand in a windbreak, an area where scrap lumber was piled, and raiding her father's supply, the "precious" nails were then wrapped in paper that previously had lined fruit crates.[52]

Some camp artists were forced to engage in activities they understood as bordering on stealing. Imprisoned internees risked embarrassment and further punishment by snatching wood from guarded camp lumber piles. Shuzo Chris Kato remembers gathering furniture-making supplies at Minidoka as his "first venture into stealing for his family." Accompanied by friends, Kato crawled under a barbed-wire fence surrounding the lumber pile to "steal" wood for bench and table making.[53] At Poston, a Nisei teenage girl waited for the dark of night before approaching wood left by outside contractors responsible for building barracks.[54] After discovering a similar source of furniture-making materials, Kimi Yanari recruited a girlfriend, and together they conducted a nighttime raid on Rohwer's lumberyard, which was guarded by a mounted MP. Having successfully and safely secured lumber for shelf and chair making, Yanari recalled: "That was the only time I ever stole anything."[55] At dusk each night, occupants of Minidoka's bachelors' barracks looked out their windows toward the camp storage area to "literally see lumber walking off in many directions."[56] In addition to threats presented by armed guards, open and unfinished sewer ditches proved formidable obstacles to the successful completion of nocturnal lumber raids.[57]

Internal security forces comprised of internees paid by the War Relocation Authority were most often responsible for protecting lumber piles, so tensions were to be expected. These security officers were accused by other internees of being inu, translated as "dogs," and collaborating with camp administrators. Members of Poston's security force patrolled in marked cars, prompting angry internees to scratch off the PO from POLICE, leaving the letters LICE on the vehicles.[58] Although George Fukasawa preferred to ignore the wood-gathering activities of his fellow internees, as a Manzanar security guard he often found himself in the awkward position of protecting government property in the form of lumber.[59] Internees were not always so lucky to encounter men like Fukasawa, as evidenced by the shooting of a Japanese American man by a U.S. Army soldier guarding Manzanar's lumber pile.[60]

Shortages of furniture-making material had reached crisis proportions at Tule Lake when frustrated and desperate internees swarmed a delivery truck loaded with lumber and then carted off the contents. Having witnessed this incident, Noboru Shirai commented: "Those who knew the truck drivers and lumberyard workers got what they wanted. Nobody else did, since polite requests were always denied."[61] After being caught removing lumber designated for building a barracks that would serve as Manzanar's hospital, five members of a boys' "gang" were admonished by the camp director, to the great embarrassment of their parents.[62] As late as May 1943, a full eight months after opening,

Paul Taylor, the head administrator of the Jerome camp in Arkansas, warned Japanese Americans that taking lumber from "construction areas" was punishable by forced labor without compensation and a jail sentence. Apparently, the irony of being threatened with further imprisonment while already incarcerated was lost on some War Relocation Authority officials.[63]

Furniture was only one art form used by internees to transform their living units into places of survival. With the basic and immediate need for beds and furniture met, women resisted oppressive living conditions in assembly centers and concentration camps by crocheting, sewing, weaving, embroidering, and knitting. Colorful and intricately crocheted blankets, tablecloths, teapot holders, and pillowcases were popular and welcome additions to drab surroundings. Needlecrafters who created decorative arts for living units often worked together, sharing techniques and ideas. Women imprisoned in Tanforan created "house-step sewing circles" in which they made a wide range of items with yarn and fabric, including table runners, slipcovers, lamp shades, bedspreads, afghans, and quilts. Tulare women discovered it was possible to crochet colorful rugs from discarded rags.[64] Embroidered and carved landscapes served as colorful wall hangings at Heart Mountain, with one women taking advantage of the administration's efforts to develop a ceramic factory. On a thick slab of clay, she carved out the defining element of Heart Mountain's landscape in the background and sculpted a group of residential barracks in the foreground. By kiln firing the panel to a temperature that allowed liquid glaze to be applied without dissolving the clay, this crafter was able to highlight her design with colors.

At Rohwer, an old loom requiring repairs sat unused for several months, but a newly hired staff person with weaving skills was eager to restore the device to working condition. Soon imprisoned women were unraveling burlap sacks retrieved from camp warehouses, washing and coloring the "yarn" with vegetable dyes, and then weaving the material into rugs. Other artists gathered flat slender sticks and wove them into

4. Embroidered landscapes served as colorful wall hangings at Heart Mountain. Photographer: Tobie Matava. Courtesy of the Heart Mountain, Wyoming, Foundation.

Venetian-like blinds for windows, and when bundles of clothes were donated to the camp, internees cut them into strips to create more than seven hundred rag rugs for the floors of living units.[65] Women imprisoned at Topaz created stuffed animals from percale or gingham and used worn out sweaters and blankets as filling. Patterns for pandas and giraffes that stood a foot high were provided by the women's page editor of the

5. Carved clay tablet depicting the Heart Mountain landscape. Photographer: Tobie Matava. Courtesy of the Heart Mountain, Wyoming, Foundation.

camp newspaper, who informed her readers that these bed or shelf decorations were easily made for ten cents' worth of materials and doubled as
toys for children.[66] Internees lucky enough to have teapots were offered
patterns for creating potholders in the likeness of a horse, made with
black-and-white-checkered percale and red bias trim.[67] Another Topaz
woman solved a persistent cold weather problem by crocheting woolen
covers that prevented her family's hands from adhering to frigid metal
doorknobs. According to her seventeen-year-old daughter, losing a piece
of flesh while opening doors was a frequent and painful experience before
her mother's invention.[68] Such practical additions to living quarters were
carefully created to brighten the austere interior surroundings.

Daughters and mothers, hoping to improve their living quarters,
browsed through the Sears and Roebuck and Montgomery Ward catalogs for material and together sewed draperies.[69] Fifteen years old at the
time of her transfer from Santa Anita, a daughter remembered helping
her mother sew draperies to make their Amache, Colorado, unit more
"comfortable."[70] A Topaz mother and her two young daughters mail-
ordered pink fabric and hand sewed curtains and covers for recently
made shelves.[71] Imprisoned without their father and husband, who had
been taken into custody by FBI agents on the night of December 7, 1941,
this family of three females furnished their living unit with the help of a
man and his son living in the same block. Draperies served functional as
well as decorative purposes. When frequent noises from barrack mates
awakened a young Puyallup girl, she appreciated curtains made by her
mother because they blocked out the powerful beam of the search lights
manned each night by armed U.S. soldiers in guard towers. Once shipped
to her permanent location of imprisonment, this same girl helped her
mother pick out white organdy fabric from a catalog. When the material
arrived, they sewed curtains for their Minidoka living unit.[72]

Artificial flowers were also frequent additions that made living
quarters more hospitable. Careful to save colorful pages from catalogs
and magazines, women transformed the paper into flowers and then

sewed them onto muslin-covered balls stuffed with waded paper, sewing scraps, or discarded bedding materials. Measuring approximately six inches in diameter, these artificial flower arrangements were hung from ceilings and walls of living units. Other women created similarly flowered artwork from silk scraps.[73] Women imprisoned at Poston made artificial chrysanthemums, gardenias, iris, sweet peas, cherry blossoms, lilacs, and carnations from colored paper that once lined apple and orange crates. One teenage girl described artificial flower making as the "latest rage" but personally found making carnations a "tedious experience."[74] A reporter for Heart Mountain's newspaper observed that "dexterous feminine fingers" were making up for the absence of greenery and flowers by making roses from crepe paper purchased through mail order catalogs and wire gathered on scavenging trips. In spite of its sexist characterizations, this statement is evidence of the difficulties encompassing artificial flower making. New to the art form, Miwako Oano described her friend's flowers as "so beautiful and so realistic that when I come home every day, my first impulse is to inhale the sweet fragrance one would expect to find emanating from such loveliness."[75]

Ikebana was an art form commonly practiced in all ten concentration camps, and its results lined shelves and rested on tables in the living quarters of internees. Dating back to the sixth century and finding its origins in the diverse range of plant life offered by Japan's geography and climate, ikebana is a generic name for many schools and styles of Japanese flower arranging. Early ideas about arranging flowers were introduced in Japan by Chinese Buddhists, who presented their creations as religious offerings to the dead and alter adornments. However, the formalization and theoretical development of ikebana occurred in Japan, beginning in the sixteenth century with the Ikenobo school, which demanded that artists adhere to a strict set of rules. Since this time varying styles have emerged, such as rikka (standing flowers), seika (living flowers), nageire (flowers thrown in bowl-shaped vases), and moribana (flowers piled in low vases or shallow dishlike containers). Distinctive schools shaped by historical, social,

6. Artificial flowers made at Manzanar, June 30, 1942. Photographer: Dorothea Lange. Courtesy of the National Archives and Records Administration.

7. Artificial roses made at Manzanar. Courtesy of the Eastern California Museum.

and cultural contexts also developed, among them the modern schools of Ohara and Sogetsu, established in 1910 and 1930, respectively. Reacting to the rigidity of Ikenobo, the Ohara school offered more room for individual creativity by advancing the idea that arrangements were vehicles through which artists could express their feelings for flowers. Emerging during the 1930s, the Sogetsu school broke all ties with traditional rules, conceptual theories, and botanical restrictions by incorporating dead branches and withered leaves among many other materials.

At risk of over simplifying this complex and deeply theoretical art form, ikebana is grounded in the belief that the lives of flowers and the lives of humans are inseparable. The style, size, shape, texture, and color of both arrangements and containers carry great meaning. In addition to using empty space to communicate ideas, ikebana artists attach significance to the location of arrangements and the occasions for which they are created. Along with flowers, a great diversity of materials have been used since the 1930s, including but not limited to branches, vines, leaves, grasses, berries, fruit, seeds, and dried or wilted plants, with each conveying a meaning of its own. With the knowledge that a wider range of methods and materials was gaining acceptance, imprisoned Japanese Americans likely found it easier to adapt even traditional styles of Ikenobo to the plant life provided by their barren environments and the paucity of vases and containers.[76]

Imprisoned at Rohwer, Mrs. Hirahara relied on branches, leaves, and plants found in the Arkansas woods and arranged her creations in a variety of rectangular cooking dishes. With the arrangements completed, the dishes were then placed in decorative boxes made from packing-crate boards. Husbands or male friends of flower arrangers often retrieved the empty crates from camp warehouses and then cut the boards to precise specifications before carefully carving, sanding, and staining the boxes. On one of her ikebana gathering trips, Hirahara came upon a recently felled red oak and was able to gather branches from the exposed stump. Focusing her arrangement around these branches, she added other wild plants and created an arrangement with green leaves that continued to

8. An example of ikebana from Jerome, November 25, 1942. Photographer: Tom Parker. Courtesy of the National Archives and Records Administration.

grow for several weeks.[77] Mrs. Homma, a teacher of ikebana at Heart Mountain, became known for her arrangements made with wild juniper, which she often displayed on a special shelf in her living unit. Relying on other wild plants and flowers indigenous to northwest Wyoming, Homma offered ikebana classes to adults and children alike.[78]

Internees at Tule Lake lived under the strictest security restrictions of all the camps because, in fall 1943, the War Relocation Authority designated

Tule Lake the segregation center for "troublemakers." Because the physical movement of all the camp's internees was severely restricted, flower arrangers at Tule Lake gained permission for a designated "procurement clerk" to gather materials outside the boundaries of the camp. Each day an internee cleared by administrators searched within a one-mile perimeter of the barbed-wire fence, collecting cattails, wild plums, tule grasses, willows, and sagebrush. Soon, however, these supplies were exhausted, so internee crafters once again approached the camp director and, with the support of a War Relocation Authority staff member, gained permission to make supervised visits to the Modoc Forest located approximately an hour east of camp. Here Tule Lake's flower and plant arrangers found an inexhaustible supply of cedar, mahogany, pine branches, and sagebrush[79]

As a Nisei teenager Molly Nakamura was first exposed to ikebana while imprisoned at Tule Lake, California.[80] A senior at Marysville Union High School when President Franklin D. Roosevelt signed Executive Order 9066, Nakamura was denied the opportunity to participate in her graduation ceremony and instead received a diploma in the mail at her Yuba City, California, home. In July 1942 Nakamura, along with her parents and younger brother, were shipped to Tule Lake, where she immediately began working as a mess hall waitress. But Nakamura's primary focus became learning ikebana, making certain to attend classes and practice the art of flower arranging. Nakamura was a committed student of ikebana and developed what would become a lifelong interest in this art form. Returning to Marysville, California, after her release, Nakamura earned her credentials as a teacher of the Ikenobo school and in 1959 cofounded the Sacramento chapter of Ikebana International, an organization that paired an interest in art with fostering international peace.

Around the same time that Nakamura began taking ikebana classes at Tule Lake, Shigeno Nishimi arrived there as a credentialed teacher of this art form.[81] Nishimi also worked as a mess hall waitress but managed to carve time from her busy schedule to offer ikebana classes. Hoping to escape the life of rice farmers, Nishimi and her new husband immigrated to the United States in 1924. After settling into life as the spouse of an antique and art dealer in Los Angeles, Nishimi began taking ikebana classes from Senka Okamoto and became a credentialed teacher of the art form before her internment. While she was imprisoned first at Walegra, also know as the Sacramento detention facility, and later at Tule Lake, she relied on local plant life, which she compared to igusa (a strawlike plant used to make Japanese tatami mats) and futoi (also a plant that produced strawlike material), and substituted artificial creations made from colored paper for fresh flowers.[82] Her arrangements were often distinguished by the use of daikon (a large white radish) and carrots. She also fostered close relationships with carpenters imprisoned at Tule Lake, who supplied her students with nails and wood to create containers for their artwork.

Released from Tule Lake in January 1946, Nishimi and her family moved to Sacramento. They were forced to abandon hopes of returning to Los Angeles because their house had been confiscated by neighbors who offered to serve as landlords during the war years. In a story all too common among Japanese Americans forced into the concentration camps, the Nashimas had all of their property and possessions stolen, an offense made possible by a series of machinations supported by the mayor of Los Angeles, who assured the U.S. Representative from California John Tolan, on April 27, 1942, that "property within this city formerly occupied or used by the Japanese will not remain idle."[83] Forty-three-year-old Nishimi adjusted to life in Sacramento by teaching ikebana classes and caring for her children and husband, who developed a general contracting business. During several trips to Kyoto, Nishimi continued her training as a master ikebana teacher and mentored aspiring artists until 1993. According to her 1997 obituary, Nishimi was known in Sacramento as a highly respected teacher of ikebana and a talented artist. Her reputation was further enhanced by a fifteen-year term as president of the Ikenobo Ikebana Society of Northern California.[84]

Kobu was an art form practiced in most of the imprisonment locations, but it was especially popular in the Arkansas camps. With an abundance of recently felled trees at their disposal, Japanese Americans imprisoned at Rohwer and Jerome decorated their living units with natural formations found in the roots of elm, hickory, and oak trees as well as with art carved from segments of tree trunks. Carefully stripping away decaying pieces of wood and bark by boiling roots and tree trunks, internees revealed raw sculptures, which were oiled, polished, and finally varnished to a high gleam.[85] Some of these artists were purists who only slightly altered figures shaped naturally, whereas others took more a aggressive approach by carving such items as match holders, bowls, and plaques from hollowed-out slabs of tree trunks. Among the natural forms were monkeys, lizards, birds, and human figures. What internees refereed to as "cypress knees" were also valued by kobu artists in that the formations often provided pieces of wood that were easily hollowed into vases. Exceptionally prized and rare, these works of art were used as vessels for flower arrangements by ikebana enthusiasts.[86]

A primary obstacle for most imprisoned crafters was overcoming persistent shortages of art-making supplies, but bon-kei enthusiasts were surrounded by two materials commonly used in their art form, sand and dirt. Perhaps best translated as "landscape in a tray," bon-kei reproduced in miniature all elements of a specific landscape, including buildings and people. Mrs. Ninomiya had been exposed to this art form during her childhood in Japan, so when she looked out on Amache's dusty landscape, she saw possibilities that eluded most internees. After completing an example of bon-kei during her first days of imprisonment, Ninomiya soon found herself with ninety-two students, none of whom had previous experience with the art form. Tray-making materials presented the biggest obstacle, with Ninomiya's pupils always on the lookout for discarded vegetable crates, but unfortunately demand far exceeded supply. Internees started a letter-writing campaign that sent friends back home off on tray-shopping expeditions, with the final stop being the post office. After they began receiving tray-making materials in the mail, Amache artists created mountain, desert, seacoast, and "imaginary Japanese" scenes. Bon-kei

9. Kobu was a popular art form in the Arkansas camps. Courtesy of the Rosalie Santine Gould Collection.

decorated many of Amache's living units, with internees mulling over the irony of making art from sand—a material they so often cursed.[87]

Freestanding wood sculptures were carved by camp crafters and placed on tables and shelves in the living units, and embroidered landscapes decorated rough barrack walls. Artwork created by imprisoned children were welcome additions to living units, with drawings and paintings sometimes covering entire sections of a wall. Internees marked holidays by creating special pieces of art. One teenager, hoping to brighten the mood of his family's first Christmas at Tule Lake, spent his monthly clothing allowance of $3.50 to purchase several packages of construction paper. After transforming green paper and glue into a one-foot-tall Christmas tree, he created ornaments by cutting small circles from sheets of red, yellow, pink, and orange paper. Once these decorations were pasted on the tree, the family of this Nisei artist admitted that the camp-made Christmas tree helped lift the "dark clouds" hanging over their lives.[88]

10. A bon-kei and ikebana display at Amache, September 11, 1942.
Photographer: Joe McClelland. Courtesy of the National Archives and
Records Administration.

Internees extended their experiences of creating livable inside places of
survival beyond the confines of their individual living units. Nameplates
and mailboxes helped internees more easily identify their living units, a
difficult task considering that blocks were laid out in standardized grids
composed of twelve identical barracks, each one indistinguishable from the
other. Assembly center structures were characterized by more variation in
style and materials, but in both temporary and permanent camps, internees
created a wide range of nameplates to distinguish their living units from
those of their many neighbors. Nameplates and mailboxes were especially
important in the early days, before gardens and landscaping took hold, creating more diversity in the landscape and differences among neighboring
barracks and blocks. Because the layout of the housing was standardized,
losing one's way was a frequent, frustrating, and sometimes traumatic

11. Nameplates helped internees distinguish their living unit from that of their neighbors at Amache, October 1945. Photographer: Hikaru Iwasaki. Courtesy of the National Archives and Records Administration.

experience, especially for youngsters and the elderly. On their first night at Heart Mountain, a group of internees wandered out among the hundreds of black tar-papered barracks in an attempt to locate the latrines, only to get lost and then rescued by a more experienced neighbor.[89] Becoming disoriented in this physical maze was not an infrequent occurrence, as noted by a woman imprisoned first at Tanforan and then Topaz: "All the residential blocks looked alike; people were lost all the time."[90]

A group of bachelors sharing a room in area C of Puyallup used scrap lumber to create an "entry roof" over the doorway and a sign identifying their living unit as the "Outside Inn." Intended as a reference to the shoddy construction common in all camps, the sign perfectly described the ability

12. A nameplate made from woven cotton yarn at Amache, October 1942. Photographer: Hikaru Iwasaki. Courtesy of the National Archives and Records Administration.

of internees and camp administrators walking by outside the barrack to gaze through gaping holes into individual living units.[91] A few signs were carved or written in Japanese, evidence that some internees were willing to closely identify with Japanese culture under especially perilous conditions. But there was conflict among internees about writing in Japanese. A young Nisei man interned at Tanforan was disturbed after noticing that a newly placed nameplate was written in Japanese, which he felt "gave our Block a Japanese name." The offended internee quickly removed the nameplate, even though he was being watched by a "couple of Kibei boys," who protested his action.[92] Mine Okubo remembered that nameplates written in Japanese were prohibited by camp administrators, which likely explained this internee's courage in removing the sign even in the presence of objectors. Other internees imprisoned at Tanforan named their living units Inner Sanctum, Stall Inn, and Sea Biscuit, sarcastically referring to the cacophonous living conditions and the animal identities of previous inhabitants. On Okubo's door was a sign reading QUARANTINE, signifying her desire for peace and quiet.[93] Burlap and tree limbs were popular nameplate-making supplies at Santa Anita, the largest and longest occupied of all fifteen temporary facilities, imprisoning over 19,000 Japanese Americans. Accompanying one nameplate was a doll made of burlap, sitting on a tree branch, with wood shavings for hair and buttons for eyes.[94]

Concentration camp barracks were made of cheap, unseasoned wood, usually pine or redwood, and black tar paper, creating a maze of replicas that internees found difficult to navigate. An Amache widow and her seven children decided on Sleepy Lagoon as a fitting name for their living quarters and carved the letters into a slab of wood. Mas Ueysugi, who was seventeen years old at the time of imprisonment, later commented that the nameplate gave their unit a "homey atmosphere."[95] Creating anything resembling a home must have presented a formidable task considering that Amache, laid out on a north–south grid, was a one-mile-square area of 10,500 acres. A thirty-block internee housing area—with each block made up of twelve barracks measuring 20 by 120 feet each, and each barrack further divided into six equal units—was separated by barbed wire from the upgraded staff housing area. Building materials for Amache's internee living units varied from those of other camps, with asbestos shingles and fiberboard substituted for the usual tar-paper construction. A letter-number system identified specific blocks by indicating the street intersection at a block's northwest corner. Living in unit 8F, also known as Sleepy Lagoon, the Ueysugi family was two blocks from the elementary classrooms, a fortunate location for a family of seven children, especially on frigid and windy winter days in southeastern Colorado, where temperatures often dipped to thirty below zero.[96]

For the nearly 8,500 Jerome internees living in a rectangle comprised of thirty-six blocks of twelve identical barracks each, nameplates and mailboxes were powerful honing devices that allowed living units to be more easily located while also commenting on everyday internment experiences.[97] On the door of the Jerome living unit, identified by administrators as block 28, barrack 6, unit C, hung a plate with the names Mr. and Mrs. M. Nishi painted at the top and a service star in the center honoring their son George, a staff sergeant in the U.S. Army. Surrounding the service star were the names of their four daughters,

Seiji, Grace, Matsie, and Mary. At 9–7-E, a knot in the center of a polished wood board served as the letter O in the printed blue inscription,
"Generally Knot Inn," and marked the living quarters of the Tamura
brothers, Spud and John.[98] Internees approaching 12–8-D were greeted
with a more practical marker of place that included the instructions
"Please Clean Your Shoes Before Entering this Room. This Also Means
the People Living In this Room. Thank you, the boss." A designer of one
Topaz nameplate used a metal band that had been wrapped around a
large wooden packing crate, bending and shaping the long strip into his
name, Higashida. Once completed, the strip was attached to a slab of
scrap wood and placed on the living unit door.[99]

Mailboxes were also effective markers of place, with Jerome's newspaper reporting in February 1943 that "practically every" living unit
was "sporting" a mailbox of some sort.[100] Eddie Imasu made a wooden
box from spare pieces of pine and then painted the front to look like
a letter addressed to himself, including intricate drawings of a stamp
and postmark. At the Tsukamotos' living unit, internees working as
mail deliverers were required to "punch the face of Hitler" before gaining access to an opening that accepted letters and packages. Another
imprisoned Japanese American made a log cabin mailbox from small
twigs, bamboo sticks, and pieces of rough bark. When completed, the
door of the log cabin opened to accept letters, while the roof lifted to
provide ample space for packages. Smaller and less elaborate mailboxes
were made from paper milk cartons and carved from wood, with mail
deliverers leaving notes for internees to pick up larger packages at mess
halls or camp post offices. Some crafters printed names in Japanese,
others used English lettering, and many announced the inhabitants of
living units in both languages.[101]

Removed from their homes and familiar environments, internees
endured a severe form of displacement. Their dislocation was made even
more difficult by confinement in physical places characterized by hundreds of indistinguishable buildings arranged in identical patterns and
situated in monochromatic landscapes, with climates hostile to people

accustomed to lush coastal geographies. At the risk of trivializing the traumas of internment, I suggest that contemporary readers compare the experience of finding a living unit in one of these camps with that of identifying your vehicle in a 540-acre (the size of the central portion of Manzanar) parking lot filled with cars of the same make, color, model, and year.[102] Although this example does not begin to encompass the everyday obstacles experienced by imprisoned Japanese Americans, it hints at one task encountered many times each day by internees attempting to live life at the most basic level. With all blocks and barracks externally indistinct, camp-made nameplates and mailboxes were welcome additions and made losing one's way a less frequent occurrence.

Inside places such as mess halls, classrooms, hospitals, and spaces of worship also drew the attention of many camp artists. Skills and ideas developed to enhance family living units were transferred to places more firmly defined and understood in terms of shared use. Sixty-one-year-old Kamekichi Kawasaki responded to Heart Mountain's shortage of mess hall eating utensils by carving and polishing one thousand wooden spoons or shakushi from discarded apple crates. By May 1943, his efforts were shifted to creating mayonnaise spoons and chopsticks. As the *Heart Mountain Sentinel* reported: "Garbed in overalls, winter underwear sleeves rolled up, dreaming maybe of home back in sunny California, he works—unpaid and unheralded."[103] Mess hall walls were popular spaces for imprisoned artists to display their work. Amache's rough interior walls were particularly well known for hosting a wide range of wood panels carved by imprisoned Japanese Americans. After standing in long lines three times each day, internees sitting down to often meager meals were greeted by carvings, ikebana, watercolors, and embroidery among many other art forms.[104]

Christmas was a time when mess halls served as a welcoming canvas for crafters. Rohwer's landscape provided trees that internees cut down and placed in mess halls. Crafters gathered canning jar rims, which they stuffed with round balls of red cellophane. Other internees, with needle and thread, strung together dried fruits and vegetables grown in camp gardens. Together these creations decorated Christmas trees.[105]

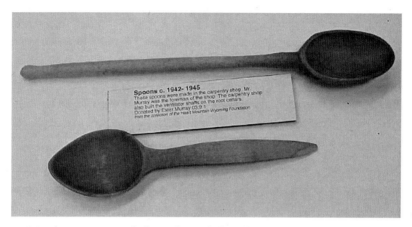

Spoons c. 1942- 1945
These spoons were made in the carpentry shop. Mr.
Murray was the foreman of the shop. The carpentry shop
also built the ventilator shafts on the root cellars.
Donated by Ester Murray 03.9.1
from the collection of the Heart Mountain Wyoming Foundation

13. Wooden spoons made from discarded apple crates at Heart Mountain. Photographer: Tobie Matava. Courtesy of the Heart Mountain, Wyoming, Foundation.

At Heart Mountain, mess hall trees were decorated with stars cut from tin cans.[106] Creating tree decorations for Manzanar's first Christmas provided welcomed relief and focus in the aftermath of the December 7, 1942, conflict between U.S. soldiers and imprisoned Japanese Americans, which resulted in the deaths of two internees and the wounding of nine others. After fourteen days of martial law, with armed guards patrolling the camp in jeeps mounted with machine guns and liberally using tear gas, segments of the traumatized population at Manzanar attempted to extract some level of normalcy by gathering scrap materials and creating Christmas decorations. Many internees spent their first days of "freedom" from martial law gently bending and then linking discarded toothbrush handles into rings to create colorful chains for encircling Christmas trees placed in all thirty-six mess halls. Once submerged in hot water, the handles became pliable and easily shaped. Other internees folded and cut intricate decorations out of tin foil wrappers used to package cigarettes and gum, or they created tree ornaments by using nails to stencil designs on the lids of tin cans.[107]

With the support of YWCA officials, young women at many camps convinced administrators to allocate spaces for "meeting and club houses" and lost little time settling into these cramped areas by creating furniture, pillows, rugs, and curtains. As a Poston Y Girl reported to national staff members: "We have received (and not very easily too!) a whole recreation hall which we are going to call the 'Y' room." Grace Morioka concluded her letter by requesting furniture and curtain-making materials.[108] Young women at Amache also solicited the YWCA for drapery- and slipcover-making material, informing the national secretary in Denver that camp-made couches were already constructed.[109] A Girl Reserves "clubhouse" at the Canal Camp section of Gila was already furnished with camp-made couches and curtains, but Y officials requested that Tucson chapter members search their attics for spare pillow-making supplies.[110] These spaces allowed teenage girls and young women to gather together in an environment free of parental supervision, which was especially important in the context of imprisonment, where families lived together in one room and privacy was nonexistent.

Classrooms were especially bleak, with teachers walking into empty shells devoid of furniture, books, and other supplies. Many internees embraced opportunities to support the education of incarcerated youngsters by creating furniture and decorations that made classroom environments more bearable. Unable to hold classes throughout the fall of 1942 because wood-burning stoves had yet to be installed, the elementary school at Topaz reopened in December. Happy to be back in her classroom teaching second graders, a young Nisei woman, who before internment had been a student at the University of California, Berkeley, eagerly hung new curtains made by her mother. As the young teacher commented: "It was a great relief to be warm in my classroom, and the atmosphere was further improved by bright colored curtains my mother had sewn for me by hand."[111] For high school seniors forced to miss their commencement ceremonies back home, Tulare's grandstand was transformed into a graduation stage. Unattractive and heavy beams were concealed with green tree branches that had been woven together, and daisy chains made by Mr. Tanaka's artificial-flower-making class bordered the steep steps graduates climbed to receive their diplomas. A huge basket filled with camp-made paper flowers decorated the center of the stage.[112]

Children also participated in enhancing classroom environments. A class of third graders was active in transforming Topaz into a survivable place when they sewed curtains and "made flowers to make our room look like spring."[113] A group of seventh grade girls imprisoned at Poston made curtains for their classroom from material purchased by their teacher. As one of the students reported: "The new curtains and the colorful pictures which we put up on the walls add to the cheer of the room."[114] A persistent shortage of furniture in classrooms forced many children to lug chairs and benches from their living units to classes and then back each day.[115] In the mornings sixteen-year-old Aiko Tanamachi carried a portable bench made by her older brother to school and returned each afternoon to her Poston I "home" with her camp-made chair in tow. Forty-two years later Tanamachi had only to look at the scars on her legs, her embodied memorials, which had been caused by nails protruding from her make-shift school furniture, to recall this experience.[116]

Poston's students were fortunate to have a school at all in that this concentration camp near Parker, Arizona, was constructed without any consideration given to or space allotted for educating school-aged children and teenagers. With the U.S. government ignoring the educational requirements of its youngest captives and refusing to allocate lumber to volunteers willing to build schools, internees were forced to employ alternative and unfamiliar methods of construction. Using natural materials provided by the physical environment, some internees joined together to make countless adobe bricks from which school buildings were then constructed. Although working with adobe was an especially taxing and dirty job, Poston's schools were completed, albeit with great sacrifice on the part of imprisoned Japanese Americans, who worked in temperatures exceeding 115 degrees. Poston I's elementary school, located

14. Making furniture for schools at Heart Mountain, September 22, 1942.
Photographer: Tom Parker. Courtesy of the National Archives and Records
Administration.

at the west end of blocks 19 and 30, was a sophisticated group of structures that included an office, auditorium, library, covered walkways,
and ten classroom buildings. On the far west side of Poston I was the
high school, a fortunate location for the previously mentioned bench-
toting Tanamachi, who lived in block 37, barrack 11, unit C, just two
blocks east. The educational complex was composed of an office, library,
auditorium, auto and wood shop, and eight classroom buildings.[117] Once
construction was completed, furnishing the classrooms was difficult
because internees again were denied access to lumber and nails.[118]

Internees also devoted crafting time and energy to making hospitals and
churches more comfortable. With Bill Yamamoto appointed as foreman, a
group of twenty-nine Jerome men organized a "cabinet shop" in November
1942. By March, despite severe shortages of materials and tools, these men

15. School furniture made by Manzanar internees, February 10, 1943.
Photographer: Francis Stewart. Courtesy of the National Archives and
Records Administration.

had completed 1,500 desperately needed hospital items, including X-ray
stands, stretchers, pharmacist's cabinets, and test tube racks, all made from
hard gumwood or oak.[119] With the motto "we make anything made of
wood," block 6 organized their own shop of eighteen carpenters, which also
filled requests from Jerome's hospital staff.[120] Women joined in to make
hospital rooms and waiting areas more bearable with the addition of paper
flowers. Young women imprisoned in the Butte Camp section of Gila decorated hospital wards and trimmed trees for Christmas celebrations.[121] Other
internees devoted their energies to creating chairs and tables for religious
services. Intricately carved butsudans were created by Buddhists and placed
in communal locations for campwide services.[122]

As these crafting activities illustrate, creating art was a critical element
in the complicated process of place making. Uprooted and incarcerated

16. Intricately carved butsudans created by internees were used in camp-wide services. Photographer: Tobie Matava. Courtesy of the National Japanese American Historical Society.

by the U.S. government, internees carried with them, in portable spaces of art, the ability to *re*make places of survival. Imprisoned Japanese Americans used these activities and the resulting artifacts to create places of survival and achieve basic levels of physical comfort. As Martha Inouye Oye remembered of her experiences at Minidoka: "Comfort was uppermost in the minds of the people when they first arrived here. As at the assembly centers, talented and creative evacuees built partitions and furniture from discarded lumber and material picked up around the barracks to make their rooms more habitable."[123] Through these efforts, internees positioned themselves in contexts of larger camp collectivities as they began sharing techniques, materials, and ideas on how to make their living units habitable. Art as a tool of recuperating a sense of place expanded as furniture makers identified internees unable to make chairs, tables, and shelves because they lacked carpentry skills or were too overwhelmed with other tasks. Needlework projects such as crocheted blankets, quilts, and pillows also addressed needs to establish minimal levels of comfort. Expanding their focus beyond the confines of individual living units, internees used art to alter inside communal places such as mess halls, classrooms, and hospitals.

In their efforts to create physical comfort, internees laid the groundwork for remaking mental and physical landscapes of survival by using art to decorate their living quarters. Stripped of their personal possessions, internees demonstrated their commitment to survival by inhabiting their living units with art in the form of kobu, wood carvings, ikebana, embroidered wall hangings, and paper flowers. Camp-made crafts articulated fluid, shifting, and multiple stances against oppressive living conditions. By filling their living units with art, internees made their surroundings look and feel less like spaces of incarceration, an important consideration for parents who struggled to establish even limited amounts of normalcy for their children. Living quarters evolved into vital places made more meaningful by camp-made and displayed art that created visual discourses controlled by internees. Through and with art, internees spoke loudly, voicing their commitment to survival by improving their material lot in life and remaking both physical and mental landscapes. In this way art aided internees in developing understandings of themselves as agents of their own lives. By remaking inside places of imprisonment, internees identified with each other on the basis of survival and comfort. By using art forms to create items such as nameplates and mailboxes, they countered conditions of dislocation and fears of being lost.

CHAPTER 3

Re-territorializing Outside Spaces

Perhaps more dramatic than interior changes to internee living quarters and shared gathering places was the rearticulation of outside living spaces. Internees re-territorialized the camps, a process of altering hostile and unfamiliar landscapes into arenas of identity articulation in which differences are declared and subjectivities enacted.[1] Through this process of re-territorialization, imprisoned Japanese Americans became anchored in unfamiliar, harsh, and antagonistic environments. These places of imprisonment were spatial expressions of race based on the U.S. government concentrating persons of Japanese ancestry in specific geographical sites. But internees altered the spatial order of these physical landscapes by joining aesthetics with politics and engaging with the art forms of gardening and landscaping as strategies for creating survivable places. For the internees, vegetable, fruit, and rock gardens as well as skating rinks, golf courses, and swimming pools were, in the words of Akhil Gupta and James Ferguson, "conceptual and political acts of re-imagination."[2] These acts of re-imagination were particularly important for many imprisoned Japanese Americans as they drew on the physical landscape to reshape understandings of power and generate new ideas that better ensured their survival.

Through the process of re-inscribing the physical environment with gardening and landscaping projects, internees imagined and enacted portable senses of place. When studying these art activities of Japanese Americans, we learn that place, even when denied by the almost limit-less power of a nation-state, can reside in portable spaces such as art. Understanding gardening and landscaping in these terms helps us see how internees identified with one another by creating portable senses of place, which they carried with them. This portability problematizes the attachment of culture to physical locations structured by nation-states and instead suggests a more transnational understanding of identity formation. Identities unmoored from physical boundaries of nation-hood, such as that of being Japanese or American or any combination of the two, appear equally relevant or powerful as identities constructed by structures of the nation-state and issues of territory. A critical tool of survival for imprisoned Japanese Americans was creating understand-ings of place as portable and then engraving this newly constructed knowledge onto the outside spaces of concentration camps.

This form of physical place making took on added meaning and importance for a people who collectively possessed a long and heteroge-neous history of geographical displacement that encompassed a series of voluntary, coerced, and forced movements. Sex, class, ethnic, religious, occupational, and generational differences constructed distinct paths of migration for many internees before they were forcibly removed from designated West Coast exclusionary areas during spring 1942. However, people of Japanese ancestry living in the United States now shared con-finement in concentration camps defined by race. Understandings of place as portable took on even more meaning when we recall that these new prisoners of the U.S. government were first incarcerated in tempo-rary facilities and later moved to more distant, permanent locations of imprisonment. Denied places of their own, Japanese Americans relied on the portable spaces of art in the form of landscaping projects to recuper-ate and remake new senses of place.

Almost immediately, internees reacted to the traumas of internment by working with soil surrounding their living quarters. As they engaged with the art form of gardening, imprisoned Japanese Americans altered the barren and dusty physical landscapes of the camps into places marked by flower, vegetable, and rock gardens complete with ponds and waterfalls. Larger landscaping and architectural additions included bridges, wishing wells, sizable seating areas, and lakes where model boat "regattas" frequently occurred, not to mention newly constructed baseball fields, skating rinks, sumo rings, and golf courses. Personal gardens were the most immediate sign of this re-territorialization process, with children and adults alike staking out small lots near their living quarters and preparing the less than hospitable soil for planting during their first difficult days of imprisonment.

Many internees were deeply effected by the bleakness of their temporary imprisonment sites, or what the government euphemistically called "assembly centers." Mary Tsukamoto, a young mother imprisoned at Fresno, was no exception. Tsukamoto was shipped by train from her home in Florin, California, to the Fresno County Fairgrounds, which she reported was hot, dusty, and devoid of greenery. The main feature at Fresno—just over a hundred tar-papered barracks—housed more than 5,000 internees between May 6 and October 30, 1942. By early June of that year, however, vegetable gardens began appearing, and within three months a community garden was providing vegetables for imprisoned Japanese Americans eating in communal mess halls. In October, when Fresno's internees were ordered to board trains destined for Jerome, Arkansas, Tsukamoto glanced back at a "transformed" landscape to see morning glory vines covering the barracks and an array of vegetable and flower gardens. Strengthened by these physical alterations, this twenty-eight-year-old Nisei mother gathered her anxious family for an exhausting four-night, five-day train trip to the Mississippi River Delta region in southeastern Arkansas.[3]

Newly created gardens evoked similar ideas and emotions from internees incarcerated at other temporary imprisonment facilities. Pausing in front of her Tulare living quarters located at block L, barrack 8,

17. Internees quickly transformed the areas around their living quarters: Tanforan on arrival, April 29, 1942 (above) and six weeks later, June 16, 1942 (right). Photographer: Dorothea Lange. Courtesy of the National Archives and Records Administration.

unit 3, an Issei woman admired a recently planted garden full of morning glories, zinnias, and green beans. Commenting in her diary about the persistence and dedication of Tulare's gardeners, she found hope in the art of others, while also noting that these gardens encompassed frustration, futility, and sorrow. Evoking ideas of dislocation, loss, and economic exploitation, she concluded her June 5, 1942, entry by writing: "Raising these products was their life. As much as they yearn, they can no longer till the acreage they had in normal times."[4] This admirer of Tulare gardens reveals how oppositional and what we sometimes think of as exclusionary ideas such as oppression and resistance, joy and sorrow, often reside together and are experienced simultaneously. The uplifting effects of gardens were also recognized by Santa Anita internees, who described

the re-territorialization of soil surrounding the living units that had once housed animals. Areas formerly trampled into fine dust by the constant traffic of race horses were being taken over by budding flowers, plants yielding vegetables, and an array of carefully nurtured greenery.[5]

Tanforan's gardeners were especially prolific, with everyone from elderly Issei to youngsters caring for newly planted vegetable and flower gardens. Although internees were aware that Tanforan was a temporary imprisonment facility, efforts to re-territorialize the camp by creating more elaborate landscaping projects were immediate with the addition of ponds and a community garden. Some personal gardens reflected a strong Japanese cultural influence, as was the case of a plot located in the infield of Tanforan's racetrack that featured a "bamboo-like" fence and Japanese lanterns. However, most gardens were characterized by rows of vegetables surrounded by a few flowering plants.[6] Three days after arriving at Tanforan, the second youngest of eight Kikuchi siblings was tending the family's "victory garden." Waiting for the coolness of

18. Garden in front of a Tanforan barrack, June 16, 1942. Photographer: Dorothea Lange. Courtesy of the National Archives and Records Administration.

night, this young boy stepped out of his living unit at eleven o'clock in the evening to water new seedlings.[7] By June, Tanforan's victory gardens were producing a wide variety of vegetables, including radishes, turnips, string beans, tomatoes, cucumbers, squash, and sugar peas, which mess hall cooks used to supplement canned army rations. On June 13, 1942, internees eating in mess hall 8 were treated to a potato salad, officially referred to as a "victory salad" garnished with grated vegetables from internee gardens.[8] In front of 15–9-2, a garden of special note included a small pond with four gold fish carved from carrots.[9]

Tanforan was the site of two "lakes," one a favorite of nature lovers and artists and the other a place enjoyed by model boat enthusiasts. Plans for Tanforan's North Lake were created by imprisoned architect Roy Watanabe, who conceived of the project as a "lake park" ideal for taking quiet walks and thinking.[10] By the time the lake opened in early August 1942, the project was the collaborative effort of many camp artists, who revised the original plan to include transplanted trees and plants, a footbridge, three rock gardens, a promenade, benches, playground, and sandy areas adjoining the water. Recognizing the danger that water presented for children, the builders limited the depth of the pond to an average of one foot, with marked sections on the north end reaching three feet deep. A concrete fountain connected to a secondary pool provided a dependable water source, and to further ensure that the lake remained full, internees constructed a fire tower on the lake's bank so practicing firemen could aid in maintaining the water level. Watanabe remained involved in the lake park, attempting to lure ducks from Tanforan Lake in an effort to complete his scenic vision for the project.[11] Some internees looked on in amazement at the efforts of these gardeners and landscapers, who were fully aware that Tanforan was not their final place of imprisonment. As one of the observers noted, internee gardeners "transformed a mere wet spot in the Tanforan scenery into a miniature aquatic park."[12]

What came to be known as Lake Tanforan existed before the implementation of Executive Order 9066, but internees maintained and improved this small pond, located in the Tanforan racetrack's infield, as a site for model boat enthusiasts. During twilight, and on Sunday afternoons after lunch, large crowds gathered at the water's edge to watch internees sail camp-made model boats. As part of a Fourth of July celebration, 2,000 spectators witnessed one hundred boats compete in a regatta, with winners in several classes receiving prizes of scrap lumber to continue their boat-making activities. Other competitive events featured nearly two hundred vessels ranging from simple ones carved from a slab of wood to elaborate models equipped with motors and automatic rudders. Some crafters relied exclusively on penknives to create their boats, whereas others mail-ordered planes and chisels from catalogs or asked friends back home to purchase wood-carving tools.

One of the first boats to appear was made by an Issei man from scrap wood, a discarded tin pail, and a bed sheet. With a nineteen-inch-tall mast, the vessel measured twenty-one inches long and five inches wide.

Although speed was likely the highest priority, this artist was also concerned with aesthetics in that he painted his vessel with a red, shiny enamel below the waterline, white above, and varnished the deck. As a finishing touch, the model boat builder added an American flag at the top of the mast. This crafter shaped sheets into sails, but others managed to convince women friends to part with silk dresses and slips.[13] Issei sailors outnumbered Nisei, but fathers often spent time with their sons creating new boats. As a result of these collaborations, the art form of model boat building gained popularity among youngsters.[14]

Model boats and the accompanying regattas were sometimes seen in less than positive terms, as evidenced by the June 19, 1942, diary entry of a twenty-six-year-old Nisei man, who wrote: "The Issei haven't anything else to do and I see them around all day painstakingly carving out these boats."[15] This statement likely reflected tensions surrounding a forced shift of familial authority from Issei men to the U.S. government, which unabashedly exercised control over the lives of Japanese Americans. Because Issei, especially men, were generally but often mistakenly thought of as more loyal to Japan and less suited to "Americanization," those who escaped separate incarceration in Department of Justice prisons were denied leadership roles by concentration camp administrators. Placed at the fringes of this already racially exploited group of people, Issei men and their internment activities such as boat building were often understood by fellow internees as evidence of weakness, impotence, and desperation.[16] As Gary Okihiro wrote: "The Issei represented an obsolete mentality, an old world flavor that had become distasteful; the Nisei symbolized the future—a new direction and style—in full pursuit of the illusive American Dream."[17]

A community flower garden full of blooming plants, benches, and a greenhouse was the joint effort of horticulturalists imprisoned at Tanforan. Located in the northwest corner of the camp just behind the hospital, this 150-square-foot flower project was surrounded by a six-foot-high wooden fence and produced a wide variety of specimens, including sweet peas, marigolds, asters, stocks, snapdragons, petunias, bachelor buttons, and chrysanthemums. Under the more than competent leadership of Mr. S. Takahashi, a 1913 graduate of Columbia University with a B.S. degree in agricultural economics, this garden project supplied flowers to mess halls, churches, hospital rooms, and administrative offices.[18] Internees not participating in this art form watched as Takahashi and his team of gardeners transformed what had once been Tanforan's dump into a colorful camp garden.[19] On September 9, 1942, when the first group of internees was about to be shipped from Tanforan to Topaz, one of the community gardeners appeared with a wheelbarrow full of flowers picked from the greenhouse. Hoping to soothe the feelings of his anxious neighbors, this artist handed bouquets through a fence that now separated internees boarding trains destined for Topaz from newly made friends about to be left behind.[20]

As the largest and longest occupied temporary imprisonment facility, Santa Anita was filled with a wide variety of gardening projects ranging from conventional squared-off plots of cultivated soil containing one or two varieties of flowers or vegetables to elaborate rock gardens.[21] Over 18,000 Japanese Americans were imprisoned at any given time in Santa Anita, and many of these internees contributed to gardening efforts. An entire plot of pansies adjoined barrack 37, unit 10, while 26–6 was the site of a rock garden based on a Japanese proverb. Complete with a well, wooden bucket, dwarf trees, morning glories, wind chimes made from glass, and frogs, John Doi's garden recounted the story of a girl who arrived at a well to draw water and found morning glories wound around the bucket and ropes. Rather than disturb the flowers, she traveled to a neighbor's well for water. Evidence that such creations resonated with internees was offered by the appearance of tanka and haiku poems on a wall bordering the garden.[22] For Santa Anita internees housed in areas where land or hospitable soil were scarce, tin cans provided space for planting. By July 18, George Ikeda's thriving garden was made up of fifty such cans gathered from mess hall trashcans.[23] Added to many of these personal gardens were examples of yard art, as in the case of three monkeys carved from wood during July 1942. A reporter for the *Santa Anita Pacemaker* suggested that the additions be named Adolf and Benito, with the last name provocatively left to the reader's imagination.[24]

A community vegetable garden located in the racetrack's infield was a prominent feature of Santa Anita's landscape. By early June, a group of thirty former truck farmers were quickly converting fifteen acres of previously unused land into soil capable of producing food for the over 18,000 hungry internees. At month's end, the total crops planted equaled three-quarters of an acre of radishes, an acre of beets, nine acres of spinach, and an acre and a half each of carrots, nappa cabbage, and romaine lettuce. On Friday, July 10, the appetites of internees were wetted by the first crop of radishes to be harvested, which equaled nearly 2,400 bunches, closely followed a week later by the arrival of camp-grown nappa cabbage on mess hall tables. As the *Santa Anita Pacemaker* enthusiastically reported, the initial thirty-five crates of cabbage represented only a "thinning" of the total crop, with the first picking yet to occur. Subsequent weeks were marked by the inclusion of an increasingly wider selection of vegetables in the diets of internees.[25] Remembering the poor quality of food provided by the government upon arrival, one Nisei woman imprisoned at Santa Anita noted substantial dietary improvements once the gardens began producing vegetables.[26]

After re-territorializing the neglected and barren "assembly center" landscapes, imprisoned Japanese Americans were forced to abandon their carefully nurtured gardens and confront even more challenging geographies. Combining the traumas of imprisonment with yet another experience of displacement, the U.S. government further accentuated the sufferings of Japanese Americans by shipping them to distant, isolated, and desolate concentration camps distinguished by harsh and unfamiliar geographies. After a seven-hundred-mile train trip from Tanforan, Kitty Nakagawa recalled her impression of Topaz, Utah, as "just black nothingness and dryness and I guess you might call it death." At Tanforan, internees had

19. Internees arriving at Topaz found a flat, dust-filled landscape, October 18, 1942. Photographer: Tom Parker. Courtesy of the National Archives and Records Administration.

drawn some comfort from the closeness of their homes and the familiar California climate, but the severity of west central Utah's Sevier Desert was beyond the imaginations of many. In the flat, beige, dust-filled landscape of Topaz, even meager alterations were dramatic, especially the appearance of plants, which added color to an achromatic palate.[27]

Despite doubts about the fertility of the Sevier Desert, many Japanese Americans approached the art of gardening with fervor. During the first spring at Topaz, small gardens were scattered throughout the camp and surrounded by fences made from cardboard boxes and scrap lumber. Intended to protect new seedlings from brutal dust storms that easily destroyed even the healthiest of plants, fences were constantly being repaired and refashioned to screen vegetables from the windy and dusty environment that characterized Topaz. In service to their always thirsty plants, successful gardeners spent most evenings lugging buckets filled with water from communal laundry facilities to their struggling seed-lings. Careful to use every drop of liquid, internees fashioned watering devices by puncturing the ends of tin cans with holes, then attaching these camp-made spigots at the end of a stick and dipping them into water pails. Several evenings of this backbreaking work convinced some camp artists to move their gardens to areas adjoining the laundry facili-ties, where water was more easily accessible. A group of men gained per-mission from administrators to transplant trees and bushes from beyond the confines of the camp's perimeters.[28] Following the example of their elders, two eight-year-old girls pitched in to help, as reported in the class diary of third graders imprisoned at Topaz. A drawing of a shovel, water-ing can, hoe, and snake was accompanied by an entry, written on May 28, 1943, informing readers that "June and Jane planted some rabbit brush which they found in the desert."[29]

Even with the careful attention of internees, over 15,000 newly planted trees and shrubs died during the first spring of imprisonment at Topaz. Donated by the Forestry Department at the Utah State Agricultural Col-lege, these specimens included 7,500 small trees, primarily black locusts, Utah junipers, and Siberian elms, and 10,000 small plants and shrubs. One row of moribund saplings was finished off by a group of school-bound children enjoying an impromptu game of leapfrog. Added to the many challenges of growing greenery in inhospitable soil was the garden-ing inexperience of Topaz's population, which was composed primarily of people from urban areas in California. Less than 250 professional farmers were confined in the Utah camp.[30] As one internee welcomed spring, she could not avoid expressing disappointment over the lack of greenery that accompanied warmer temperatures. Accustomed to lush California springs, this college-age woman even missed the appearance of dandelions in her family's yard, a sight she had learned to "disdain" from her father, who spent most of his free time during April digging out these weeds. Hoping to partially compensate for the lack of greenery, family members devoted themselves to nurturing a single daffodil bulb mailed by a friend, planting it in an old tin can, and watching it closely each day. When the flower bloomed, the young woman "was amazed at the pleasure even a single flower could bring" when compared to the "hard white glare of bleached sand."[31]

Describing a similar scene was fifteen-year-old Yoshie Tashima, who, after enduring six months of imprisonment at Santa Anita, was transported to Amache in late October 1942. With the eyes of a former Los Angeles resident, Tashima looked out on the windswept prairie lands of southeastern Colorado and fondly remembered the warm, plant-friendly climate of Santa Anita. Drawing from a long history of geographic displacements and farming experiences, many imprisoned Japanese Americans once again, in the words of Tashima, set to making a "nothing place" into "something beautiful." Within months, newly planted trees, vegetables, flowers, and even green lawns were added to Amache's beige landscape of sand dunes, sagebrush, and prickly pear cactus.[32] Frequent dust storms that made the barrack next-door invisible presented formidable and persistent obstacles to creating livable landscapes, but Amache's corps of gardeners did battle with these conditions by constantly watering the grounds. "Of course," as Tashima admitted, "on the windiest days there was nothing that could help us." Seventeen years old when he was imprisoned at Amache, Mas Ueysugi later recalled that many of the internees were former California farmers and accustomed to converting "marginally tillable soil" into "beautiful and productive" land. "At Amache," Ueysugi continued, "we did the same."[33]

A young Nisei fisherman from San Francisco, Mas Tanibata, was shipped to Lone Pine, California, by train and then boarded a bus for the short ride north on highway 395 to Manzanar. Greeted by one of many common dust storms, Tanibata was struck by "what a miserable place it was." Later, however, he remembered how camp artists altered the landscape by noting: "You know the barracks were really ugly but then these gardens made the camp beautiful."[34] Another Nisei arrived at Manzanar via a train trip to Bishop, where he, along with his wife, two sisters, and mother were transferred to a bus for the fifty-one-mile ride south on 395. Forcibly removed from their Boyle Heights neighborhood in downtown Los Angeles, this family was stunned by temperatures that reached over one hundred degrees during the day, then plunged into the thirties at night, and by the frequent dust storms that kept the entire landscape perpetually coated in inches of flourlike dust.[35] Manzanar's head War Relocation Authority administrator assumed his post in May 1942, but not before describing what greeted him as "ugly." In contrast, by mid-June this same official reported that "half of the barracks reveal the impulse toward decoration," with internees planting vegetable and flower gardens surrounded by "decorative" fences.[36]

20. Manzanar barrack garden, June 30, 1942. Photographer: Dorothea Lange. Courtesy of the National Archives and Records Administration.

Even the dry, sandy, sun-drenched soil of Gila and Poston, Arizona, gave way to the efforts of internees by producing a variety of vegetation. With his father imprisoned separately at Santa Fe, New Mexico, one brother already in the army when Executive Order 9066 was signed, and three other brothers working on a cattle ranch in Nevada, it was left to the eldest twenty-seven-year-old remaining son to accompany his mother and two sisters to Poston. Located 250 miles east of Los Angeles on the Colorado River Indian Reservation, Poston was organized into three separate camps, each three miles apart but enclosed by a single barbed-wire fence. Although administrators referred to these locations of imprisonment as Camp I, II, and III, internees renamed them Roaston, Toaston, and Duston, all tongue-in-check references to the extreme heat and pervasive dust.[37] Arriving at Roaston with his sisters and mother, this twenty-seven-year-old citrus and walnut farmer from Orange County "wasn't very pleased" when he saw the barren, dusty landscape, but he was relieved when internees immediately began planting shrubbery, gardens, and trees and even creating ponds, noting that the surroundings "got better all the time."[38]

Like Poston, Gila was also constructed on Native American land, the south central Arizona home of the Akimel O'odham (Pima) and Pee Posh (Maricopa) tribes. Over the objection of this Gila River Indian community, the War Relocation Authority "leased" more than 16,500 acres from the Bureau of Indian Affairs and organized a Japanese American concentration camp in two sections, the Butte and Canal camps.[39] Fifty miles south of Phoenix, Gila had a landscape distinguished by mesquite trees, creosote and bursage bushes, and cactus, but the dust and heat were most memorable in the minds of internees. A mother of two sons whose husband had already been picked up by the FBI and imprisoned at Lordsburg, New Mexico, Tsuyako Shimizu was forced to contend with this "barren desert," but she likely escaped the chronic water shortages that plagued the Butte Camp. Removed from her home near Guadalupe, a farming town in California known for growing lettuce, Shimizu was

21. Harvesting daikon at Gila River, November 25, 1942. Photographer: Francis Stewart. Courtesy of the National Archives and Records Administration.

likely imprisoned in the Canal portion, a segment of the camp made up primarily of Japanese Americans from rural areas. Butte, on the other hand, was the permanent site of imprisonment for internees arriving from Tulare and Santa Anita, who were predominantly urbanites.[40] Regardless of her specific location of imprisonment, Shimizu witnessed Gila undergo changes that were unimaginable when she first arrived. As she later recalled, "When we left the camp, it was a garden that had been built up without tools. It was green around the camp with vegetation, flowers and also with artificial lakes, and that's how we left it."[41]

Whereas the landscapes of Utah, Arizona, and the Colorado prairie presented constant challenges to gardening enthusiasts, internees imprisoned at Rohwer and Jerome found this art form easier to accomplish. On April 16, 1942, Jerome's newspaper reported that "just about every barracks" was surrounded by gardens of some sort and that many internees were constructing hot houses to protect plants from threats of a late frost.[42] Two weeks earlier the newspaper mistakenly reported that recent rainfall had improved block 17's struggling lawn. Printing a correction, the newspaper informed readers that the "socalled green lawn" was actually a "bumper crop of chives" and that the internee responsible for the garden was planning on flavoring soup with his produce.[43] A year later, internees organized a camp co-op from which sixteen varieties of flowers could be purchased. Among the most popular were roses, dahlias, gladiolas, and climbing ivy.[44] Portulaca flower seed was also abundant, having been shipped to Jerome by the American Friends Service Committee, a Quaker social justice group.

Sporting multicolored buds and dark green foliage, portulaca, more commonly known as moss rose, was a hardy plant that offered durable ground cover and was well adapted to the heat, humidity, and insect life of the Arkansas Delta. Moss rose edged the many walkways connecting block and barracks to communal facilities. Rohwer's growing environment was so opportunistic that many vegetable gardeners borrowed methods and ideas from ikebana artists, arranging and exhibiting their surplus produce in camp art shows.[45] But even internee gardeners imprisoned at Rohwer and Jerome were presented with obstacles in the form of poisonous and deadly snakes. Providing ideal habitat for water moccasins, cottonmouths, copperheads, and rattlesnakes, the damp, swampy Arkansas Delta region where Rohwer and Jerome were located was dangerous to walk through and especially perilous for people clearing land and planting gardens. In addition to the daily dangers presented by the abundance of poisonous snakes, the soil was often saturated with water and unable to support vegetation, a problem internees partially solved by constructing a canal system that drained off excess water.

Each camp encompassed its own set of challenges for gardeners, and many internees identified and linked the art form of gardening to their

22. The climate and soil conditions at Rohwer produced lush gardens, June 16, 1944. Photographer: Charles Mace. Courtesy of the National Archives and Records Administration.

emotional and physical survival. A former San Jose farmer used the warm corner of a Heart Mountain laundry room to get an early start on the short Wyoming growing season by planting beet, cucumber, and squash seeds in 250 previously discarded tin cans.[46] Other camp artists, hoping for early summer vegetables or winter flowers, nurtured individual seedlings in their living units, making daily trips to the communal laundry room for water. An Issei grandmother mail-ordered flower seeds from a catalog and then created a miniature winter garden in tin cans retrieved from mess hall rubbish piles.[47] Once spring arrived, space for gardens surrounding the barracks was soon gone, motivating 150 internees to create a "combined victory garden" on the outskirts of Heart Mountain. With the guidance of Kumezo Hatchimonji, an experienced farmer, these newcomers to the art of growing vegetables and fruits first built ditches connecting a nearby canal to their collective project and then separated the land into forty-five-by-twenty-foot lots, where thirty varieties of vegetables were cultivated.[48]

As internees settled into permanent locations of imprisonment, the art form of growing vegetables and flowers in small personal plots was accompanied by even more intense efforts aimed at creating larger community gardens and farm projects. Devoting themselves to tilling and planting larger lots of land, camp gardeners were soon producing more food than could be locally consumed. During the late winter of 1943, Jimmy Ito directed a Heart Mountain community garden project by constructing nine six-by-one-hundred-foot covered hotbeds, in which broccoli, cauliflower, cabbage, cucumber, cantaloupe, and watermelon seedlings were nurtured and later transplanted to fields on the outskirts of camp.[49] Six months earlier, Ito, along with two other internees, conducted soil tests to determine which areas of the camp were most suitable for planting, while another group of imprisoned Japanese Americans relied on the test results and past weather reports to choose seeds that would promise high-yielding crops. In early May, the camp newspaper reported that a "giant truck garden is mushrooming in the barren desert."[50]

Elderly Issei men such as Harry Tateishi, Kumezo Hatchimonji, and Sakusaburo Tokuda were responsible for preparing the formerly infertile Wyoming soil for planting. Before imprisonment, all three had been farmers in southern California's Imperial Valley and were accustomed to transforming desert and rocky land into fertile fields that produced an abundance of fruits and vegetables. Prevented from owning land by the 1913 Alien Land Law, Issei farmers were typically migrant agricultural laborers or sharecroppers. At best, they leased marginal land that had been rejected by white farmers. Fertile fields of melons, lettuce, and tomatoes resulted after years of backbreaking, labor-intensive farming that included the development of new techniques such as hot capping and brush covering, in which plants were covered with straw, paper bags, or small tentlike structures in the early spring to combat frost damage.[51]

23. Preparing the soil for spring planting at Heart Mountain, March 10, 1944. Photographer: Hikaru Iwasaki. Courtesy of the National Archives and Records Administration.

Joining the experience of these Issei farmers with the knowledge of younger college-educated agriculturalists produced harvests never before imagined in the barren desert of north central Wyoming.[52] By the end of June, nearly five hundred acres were planted with twenty-five varieties of vegetables and fruits, including cantaloupes, nappa cabbage, spinach, daikon, popcorn and sweet corn, and peas. These successful cultivation efforts were accomplished with the help of seventy-five women, who rushed to make the most of the short 119-day growing season by spending ten nonstop, backbreaking days transplanting seedlings of cucumbers, onions, eggplant, tomatoes, cantaloupes, broccoli, cauliflower, cabbage, bell and chili peppers, and celery onto sixty-five acres.[53]

Because Manzanar served as both a temporary and permanent site of imprisonment, its community gardens were not abandoned, and they benefited from the constant attention of camp artists. Guarded by soldiers in thirty-five military vehicles, the first group of Manzanar internees arrived in late May 1942, transported in a 140–passenger car caravan. After completing the 240-mile trek from Los Angeles, the vehicles were seized by the U.S. Army and used for military purposes or buried in the California desert, never to be returned to their Japanese American owners.[54] Along with the 420 Japanese Americans, the cars were stuffed to the brim with personal belongings and gardening supplies, including tomato plants, vegetable seeds, and garden tools.[55] Many Issei farmers with decades of experience cultivating leased land surrounding Los Angeles arrived at Manzanar committed to harvesting food during the first growing season and immediately organized collective garden projects. One of their first tasks was solving the water shortages that had plagued the Owens Valley region since the turn of the twentieth century, a problem camp gardeners overcame by expanding an already established system of irrigation ditches.

Located in a long narrow desert valley between the eastern slope of the Sierra Nevada and White-Inyo mountain ranges, Manzanar was founded in 1905 as a small farming community named after the Spanish word for apple. A river fed by mountain snowfields supplied an elaborate irrigation system of ditches and canals, which transformed this arid valley into a flourishing agricultural center producing corn, wheat, potatoes, alfalfa, grapes, apples, and pears.[56] Along with its twenty-five homes, town hall, schoolhouse, and general store, the town boasted nearly 5,000 apple and pear trees and a fruit-packing warehouse. While Manzanar and Owens Valley residents were harvesting record crops, 250 miles south and, more importantly, downstream of Manzanar, the city of Los Angeles was growing by 100,000 new residents each year.[57] Hoping to satisfy swelling water demands, Los Angeles city officials began purchasing property in Owens Valley for the water rights alone, and by 1933 owned 95 percent of the valley's farmland and 85 percent of the town's property. Now in complete control of the water supply, Los Angeles city officials constructed an aqueduct that effectively drained the valley dry. Without a reliable source of water, Manzanar was abandoned until the signing of Executive Order 9066.[58]

Authorized by camp administrators to work outside the barbed-wire perimeters of the camp, "rock gangs" composed primarily of male internees repaired and expanded an abandoned irrigation system by digging new ditches that funneled the runoff from the Sierra Nevadas directly into the camp. Lined with rocks, these new canals furnished water for growing fruits and vegetables. Internees who worked on these rock gangs were allowed to spend nights outside camp boundaries. Many workers seized on this opportunity to hike into the Sierra Nevadas on trout-fishing trips. These trips, along with providing fish for many good dinners, also supplied fish used to stock small garden ponds. After they established a reliable source of water, many internees worked to cut down on dust by instituting a program that provided seed, rakes, and shovels to anyone willing to plant and nurture struggling blades of grass.[59] Once seeded, these lawns were sometimes decorated with yard art, as was the case in front of block 5, barrack 6, unit 4. The caretaker of this yard, a foreman for a crew of tree trimmers, used the twisted roots and branches he gathered while working to create monkeys, penguins, and turtles. Other internees celebrated the newly constructed irrigation system by creating "hobby gardens" in firebreak areas between barracks. By early June 1943, an all-volunteer crew was caring for a flower garden planted in firebreaks 11 and 17, while a vacant area between barracks 12 and 13 in block 6 was just beginning to sprout vegetables.[60] Rock gardens with small ponds were added to the perimeters of these community gardens to provide additional living space outside the confines of the crowded barracks.

What began as a small and simple watered rock garden adjacent to one of Manzanar's mess halls evolved into a more elaborate project complete with a pond surrounded by transplanted trees, two-ton boulders, massive tree stumps, and a wishing well. Hoping to provide a respite from long mess hall lines, two cooks who worked the breakfast and lunch shifts devoted their afternoons to this garden project. The venture drew the attention of Akira Nishi, a former nursery owner from Los Angeles, who approached the two men and offered his services in creating an architectural plan that would include a large, figure-eight-shaped pond. With construction well under way, enthusiasm grew, and internees throughout the block picked up shovels and helped clear a larger area.

Another group of gardeners, supervised by guards, drove an army truck and trailer equipped with a cable winch a short distance to the Sierra Nevada foothills. Here, these camp artists gathered live trees and plants, along with boulders and large tree stumps that were later converted into seating for internees waiting in the long mess hall lines. Completion of the project was threatened when a top administrator agreed to supply a mere three bags of cement, twenty bags short of the amount required for building the pond alone. But the cook who had originally conceived of the garden was not deterred. He simply devised a plan based on presenting the original permit for three bags over and over again to warehouse managers until the required amount of cement was secured. When it was completed in early July 1942, this elaborate and collaborative garden served as a model for other Manzanar crafters, who created eighteen subsequent gardens distinguished by sizable ponds.[61]

Gardeners at Manzanar struggled together against persistent windstorms that threatened to destroy everything but fruits and vegetables grown close to the ground. Although melon, radish, and cucumber plants consistently produced small, yet edible vegetables and fruits, vine-growing vegetables such as tomatoes demanded careful placement around windbreaks and constant attention to produce even marginal yields.[62] By June 4, 1942, over 125 acres were cultivated in radishes, cucumbers, squash, tomatoes, lettuce, spinach, potatoes, cantaloupe, and watermelon, with corn used as windbreaks to protect plants from frequent and violent dust storms.[63] By summer's end, over 300 acres of camp land were producing fresh fruits and vegetables. A reporter for the camp newspaper recognized

24. Woman working in a Manzanar community garden, July 2, 1942.
Photographer: Dorothea Lange. Courtesy of the National Archives and
Records Administration.

the contributions of older internees by noting that initially only one Nisei
was involved in these collective farming operations.[64]

Internees also pruned and watered abandoned pear and apple
orchards planted at the turn of the twentieth century. By August 26, 1942,
gardeners began harvesting a yearly crop of nearly 4,000 boxes of pears
alone.[65] For one teenager who worked as the timekeeper for Manzanar's
many boiler tenders, fruit from the pear orchards located in the firebreak
between blocks 23 and 29 provided extra nourishment. Walking from
one block to another, and making two rounds daily to check in with

the men tending boilers in all thirty-six blocks, Shiro Nomura looked forward to rest breaks in the orchard, where he supplemented meager mess hall portions with freshly ripened fruit.[66] Manzanar's pear trees also held significance for seven-year-old Jeanne Wakatsuki, marking the transition from a life that was "outrageous" to one that was "tolerable." In spring 1943, Wakatsuki's family moved to block 28, which adjoined a moribund pear orchard, a location that allowed her mother to be closer to the hospital where she worked as a dietician. After experiencing a difficult year of imprisonment that had encompassed the trauma of being separated from her father, who was incarcerated for nine months at Fort Lincoln in Bismarck, North Dakota, and then living through his abusive alcoholic rages once he was reunited with his family in Manzanar, Wakatsuki was relieved when her father found a new focus that drew him outside the confines of their crowded living unit to care for a group of previously neglected trees.[67]

Wakatsuki's father continued to brew rice wine in a homemade still, using rice and canned fruit as ingredients, and the elderly man engaged in long, heated, and often violent debates with family members and fellow internees concerning how to respond to a loyalty questionnaire instituted by the U.S. government. When, however, he focused his energies on harvesting pears, his violent outbursts decreased. In addition to his orchard activities, Wakatsuki's father began building a rock garden just outside the doorway of their living unit with stones gathered from the Sierra Nevadas. He also began making furniture from myrtle limbs found on the banks of irrigation ditches and creeks.[68] As the experiences of the Wakatsuki family illustrated, creating art in the form of gardening and furniture making proved effective tools for survival. As Wakatsuki herself suggested, after moving to block 28 she could almost imagine herself at home near the Pacific Ocean because the sound of wind blowing through the leaves of revived pear trees reminded her of the surf.

At Children's Village, a facility constructed at Manzanar to house Japanese American orphans, veteran gardeners helped children landscape the grounds of their new home and plant gardens.[69] Opened on June 23, 1942, Children's Village was the government's remedy to a growing "orphan problem." Before December 7, 1941, Japanese American orphans resided in three California institutions, one of which was the Shonien, where Lillian Iida and Harry Matsumoto worked. When confronted with the possibility of dispersing the children throughout all ten camps, Iida and Matsumoto convinced representatives of the U.S. government that keeping the children together as a family unit was the least damaging option, and the two volunteered to take responsibility for all orphans at Manzanar. Added to these were children of single parents who had been arrested by the FBI and imprisoned in Department of Justice facilities, as in the case of Takatow Matsuno and his seven siblings from Terminal Island, California. A total of 101 children lived in three barracks, with the west structure housing the mess hall, meeting rooms, laundry facilities, and staff living space, and the center building serving as the nursery and girls' dormitory. Boys had the east barrack all to themselves. As a part of their continuing efforts to help the children create a livable environment in which to grow up, Issei males later added a gazebo to already completed gardens.[70]

The community gardening activities of Tule Lake uniquely encompassed layered meanings of re-territorialization. In the wake of the loyalty questionnaire and subsequent conversion of Tule Lake into a segregation center for "disloyal troublemakers," newly transferred internees refused to work in the fields and produce was beginning to spoil. One of the internees' demands was that farm production be limited to the needs of Tule Lake alone. Administration officials responded by recruiting "loyal" volunteers from other camps to harvest 300 acres of crops. An elaborate and profit-making enterprise totaling 2,900 acres, Tule Lake's agricultural system supplied produce to the U.S. Army and Navy as well as to private companies. Between November 1 and November 26, 234 Japanese Americans from other camps harvested fifty-two carloads of produce, which was immediately shipped to Gila, Amache, Minidoka, Manzanar, Heart Mountain, Jerome, and Topaz.

25. Potato planting at Tule Lake, July 1942. Photographer: Francis Stewart. Courtesy of the National Archives and Records Administration.

Nine carloads of surplus potatoes were sold to the Pacific Fruit and Produce Company. Tensions between volunteer crews and Tule Lake's community gardeners were palpable, with both groups equally motivated to employ the art of gardening to engage in a complicated process of re-territorialization.[71]

Mainstream media sources noted internees' efforts to convert barren desert land into productive soil.[72] In describing the experiences of Japanese Americans imprisoned at Poston, Arizona, a magazine reporter remarked: "The settlers looked at the jungle of tough greasewood, mesquite and cacti

that must be cleared, at the thousands of acres that must be leveled, worked
and reworked before anything could be planted."[73] Beyond the reporter's
classification of Japanese Americans imprisoned in concentration camps
as "settlers," which is more than problematic, he clearly saw the difficulties of nurturing plants of any kind in these locations of imprisonment.
A year later, another reporter visiting Poston for the *St. Joseph News Press*
observed: "Bleak and dusty at first, the center now is green with gardens,
lawns and trees."[74] The *Monitor,* a Denver newspaper, informed readers
that residents of Granada, a town near Amache, "either shook their heads
dubiously or laughed when they heard that Japanese evacuee farmers were
planting mung beans, tea, lettuce, and pascal celery." But after a year the
same newspaper reported: "They're not laughing anymore—they're looking, listening, and learning."[75]

In addition to the re-territorializing efforts of gardeners, other internees
refashioned barren landscapes into sumo rings, basketball courts, baseball
fields, swimming pools, skating rinks, and golf courses. Some internment
scholars have been hesitant to write about these projects, especially the
creation of golf courses, for fear that these re-territorialization activities
might be interpreted as evidence that internees were "pampered." But the
appearance of such art was more a testament to the efforts and skills of
internees than to humane treatment by administrators. Although golf is
usually played on lush, manicured greens and fairways, camp courses were
primarily sand, a material that was in plentiful supply at most imprisonment locations. At Manzanar, Mas Tanibata, a Nisei fisherman from Terminal Island, first developed an interest in golf while clearing sagebrush
from the firebreak area that was soon to be a very short nine-hole course.
Fairways were a mixture of coarse, unraked sand and clods of dirt, with
the so-called greens composed of fine sand that internees oiled to create a
firm, puttable surface. When, and more importantly if, balls reached the
green, a roller made up of a two-foot-long pipe attached to a handle was
dragged between the hole and ball so that putting was possible. Threaten-
ing to curtail the activities of golf enthusiasts was the expense of replacing

26. Playing golf on Manzanar's dirt- and dust-filled fairways, February 13, 1943. Photographer: Francis Stewart. Courtesy of the National Archives and Records Administration.

balls blackened by dirt- and dust-filled fairways, but this problem was soon solved when an internee ordering golf clubs from a Sears catalog also purchased a can of white paint.[76]

After completing plans for Tanforan's North Lake, Roy Watanabe turned his attention to his newest project: designing a six-hole pitch-and-putt golf course. Employed as an architect since graduating from the University of California in 1936, this prolific artist was now supervising a landscaping crew of thirty internees.[77] After he located a vacant weed patch on the grounds of Tanforan Racetrack in San Bruno, Watanabe, with the help of two other imprisoned architects, expanded his original design to include a nine-hole, par-three course. Completed in four weeks, the course opened in the middle of July and averaged forty golfers per day, 60 percent of whom were beginners.[78] With its limited room, Tanforan was a short course. Its holes ranged from between 40 to 75 yards long, but they presented challenges to even experienced golfers, who found breaking par an impossible task. Another nine-hole, par twenty-seven course was created in District A of Puyallup, a temporary imprisonment facility separated by barbed wire into four sections and located thirty-five miles south of Seattle, Washington. As one of 2,000 internees to be imprisoned in District A, Mits Kashiwagi, an experienced golfer, described the course as "interesting," an observation backed up by scores in the 50s.[79]

To outsiders, internee-constructed swimming pools may appear extravagant, but for Japanese Americans imprisoned at Poston, where temperatures frequently exceeded 130 degrees, these landscape additions were necessities. Internees in all three units established a cooperative labor system requiring each block to devote a specific number of hours to completing swimming pools.[80] Summer temperatures in Powell, Wyoming, were not as severe as those in Poston, but on days when thermometers reached above 100 degrees, an internee-made swimming pond provided welcome relief. With the permission of camp administrators, internees dug a large hole, lined it with stones, created a diving platform, and finally flooded it with water from a nearby ditch.[81] Minidoka's internees frequently swam in a canal on the north side of camp, but after a drowning occurred, two swimming pools were built.[82] An especially unique aboveground swimming pool was constructed out of wood in Area B of Puyallup. Located in a cramped space between two barracks and resembling a giant squared-off hot tub, the pool was created by a group of men to entertain children incarcerated in Area B.[83] Remembering that Puyallup was a temporary facility and open for less than five months, this re-territorialization project represented a high level of investment both in terms of time and materials.

Heart Mountain internees staked out and then flooded a large field to create an ice-skating area. The sport became an especially popular wintertime activity, and the arena a popular meeting place. Some internees saved their meager wages of $12, $16, or $19 a month to buy skates from mail-order catalogs, but with the cost of ice skates in the 1943 Sears and Roebuck catalog at $6.85, purchasing a new pair represented a considerable investment.[84] After spending most of the afternoon of January 9, 1943, watching a group of youngsters from Heart Mountain's block 1 enjoy this wintertime activity, a seventeen-year-old teenager ordered his first pair of skates. Even though his first experience produced sore arches, bumps, and bruises from his many falls, Stanley Hayami reported in his diary that skating was "still a lot of fun." His pleasure was tempered by worries about dwindling finances, but he continued to enjoy skating, a novel sport for most Heart Mountain internees, who before imprisonment had lived in the warm climate of California.[85] Internees hesitant to lace up the boots found contentment in observing the activity. As a reporter for the *Heart Mountain Sentinel* remarked, watching skaters "lifts us momentarily out of this world."[86]

Although the skating season in Utah's Sevier Desert was much shorter than that of northwestern Wyoming, Topaz internees under the supervision of Moto Takahashi built an open-air skating rink by first creating a dirt bank, then opening up the fire hydrant, and finally, waiting for the water to freeze. Just as at Heart Mountain, internees purchased skates from mail-order catalogs, as in the case of a teenage boy who surprised his sister with a long-cherished and much-enjoyed gift. Warmly remembering this gift years later, the sister wrote: "I thought that it was so nice of him and we had fun on that ice rink." Located on the south side of camp between blocks 37 and 38, the rink measured 410 by 440 feet. There, internees were able to enjoy a short yet frigid season of skating, with December temperatures hovering around zero. Sixty-one years after stepping onto the rink at Topaz, Kumiko Kariya Matsumoto recalled that skating provided pleasurable moments during a "drab and miserable" time.[87]

27. Ice-skating was a popular winter activity at Heart Mountain, January 10, 1943. Photographer: Tom Parker. Courtesy of the National Archives and Records Administration.

Baseball, basketball, sumo wrestling, football, and judo enthusiasts altered camp landscapes, with every imprisonment location including sporting areas.[88] An especially unique "tennis basketball court" was designed at Santa Anita. In preparation for their imprisonment, three San Francisco youngsters made sure that a basketball hoop was among the items accompanying them to Santa Anita. The boys, who ranged in age from thirteen to fifteen, spent their first days in camp hunting for a suitable place from which to hang their prized possession. Unsuccessful and frustrated, they devised a miniature basketball goal and net from a scavenged piece of wire and string. After nailing up this device behind barrack 28, these three buddies, along with new friends, played what seemed to observers to be endless games of "tennis basketball."[89]

Rock, pebble, and wooden walkways were common and necessary additions to all the imprisonment landscapes. This need was especially clear to internees who were unfortunate enough to arrive in the wake of frequent spring rainstorms. Tanforan's unimproved walkways were referred to as "slush alleys," with small amounts of rain causing internees to struggle through silt-like mud.[90] Stepping off a bus at Puyallup in April 1942 after a sudden spring downpour, a family of four from Seattle immediately "sank ankle deep into gray Glutinous mud."[91] One brother and sister arrived prepared for the worst after having been warned of muddy conditions by friends already imprisoned at Tanforan. The siblings, who had been forcibly removed from their home in Berkeley, California, arrived wearing boots they had recently purchased—a fortunate occurrence since they found themselves trekking through high weeds and sticky mud before they located their assigned living unit, previously identified as stable 16, stall 50. The grounds of Tanforan Racetrack were still wet from a downpour the previous day, and remained difficult and exhausting to negotiate.

After being transferred to their permanent location of imprisonment, these same siblings reported that conditions at Topaz were equally challenging, with internees carving one-foot-high getas to ensure that their feet remained mud free on walks home from the communal bathing facilities.[92] But negotiating muddy terrain in stilt-like sandals was beyond the athleticism of many Japanese Americans. And, according to Fumi Hayashi, creating walkways was a necessity because the alkaline soil at Topaz repelled water: "It stayed on top, so what we would do was we gathered rocks and make kind of a pathway up high, you know, about a foot up and then all the in between places would be full of water. We'd make these little pathways so that we could walk to the bathroom or to the mess halls

and not get all muddy."[93] For former residents of California, the first snow-
fall at Topaz was accompanied by an atmosphere of excitement. This sense
of novelty was quickly dampened by the appearance of the sun, followed
closely by melting snow, which produced sticky mud that was backbreaking for even the strongest internees to traverse.[94]

The landscapes of Rohwer and Jerome were especially challenging
because these camps were located in the swampy Arkansas Delta region.
At an elevation of 140 feet, Rohwer was laced with river inlets, and outlying
areas remained underwater during the spring months.[95] Adapting to this
geography, a group of women imprisoned at Jerome created a maze of raised
wooden walkways, with one camp administrator commenting somewhat
defensively: "Women are equal to men when it comes to digging, picking
and wielding heavy tools if not better."[96] With rock and wooden walkways
completed, internees could more easily walk to and from daily activities
and tasks without sinking ankle deep into fine layers of flourlike dust on
sunny days and muddy silt during frequent rain storms.[97] While most
internees cursed the mud, Joseph Sasaki saw possibilities in this "alluvial
muck." When not working as Jerome's optometrist, Sasaki experimented
with the mud, which he shaped into ashtrays and figurines, and then
"toasted" his creations over or in potbellied stoves. Devising reliable clay
from a mixture of various muds, he named his pottery Densonware after
the post office's official designation for the camp.[98]

Perhaps nowhere more clearly do we see the relationship between the
physical and mental, and connections between individual and collective
identity formation, than in the process of re-territorialization. Through
their efforts to remake locations of imprisonment into survivable spaces,
internees expanded their mental landscapes. Frequently employing the
word *transformation* as an apt description of the changes to their
material surroundings, some internees also articulated the edifying
and strengthening effects of physical landscapes on their minds and
emotions. At Topaz, a college-age internee was buoyed by the pleasure
she experienced when a single daffodil bulb bloomed, and some Heart

28. Walkways constructed at Rohwer helped internees avoid ankle-deep dust or muddy silt, June 16, 1944. Photographer: Charles Mace. Courtesy of the National Archives and Records Administration.

Mountain internees were "momentarily lifted" from their world of imprisonment by activities on a newly constructed skating rink. Not only did vegetable and fruit gardens create and fortify moods of survival for internees, but they also drastically improved concentration camp diets, evolving literally into embodied monuments of re-territorialization. Internee gardeners from all ten camps converted 10,000 acres of barren land into crop-producing soil, and in 1943 alone they harvested forty-one million pounds of vegetables.[99] With and on the soil, internees identified on the basis of re-territorialization to create collective art projects such as gardens, basketball courts, and walkways—all with others in mind. Re-territorialized camp landscapes became public sculptures that some internees choose to carve together out of the soil.

29. Manzanar before (top) and after (bottom), June 30, 1942.
Photographer: Dorothea Lange. Courtesy of the National Archives and
Records Administration.

Re-territorialization efforts were of course often restricted by camp administers, as in the case of an arbor created by internees living in block 17 at Jerome. Measuring twelve feet square with a ten-foot-high roof, this porchlike structure was attached to a barrack and became an especially popular after-dinner meeting place.[100] Anxious to restrict large, idle crowds of internees from gathering informally in social settings, a War Relocation Authority official ordered the arbor removed, citing it as a fire hazard. For some this reasoning was hopelessly hypocritical since camp administrators ignored the obvious fire hazards presented by the tar-papered and raw wood architecture of the internees' living units.[101] As this example illustrates, issues of territory and power were critically important to camp administrators, which made gardening and landscape projects even more essential to re-territorialization efforts. Government officials interpreted these projects as industrious and evidence that Japanese Americans were becoming "Americanized" rather than understanding gardening or improvements to camp landscapes as subversive or a challenge to the power wielded by structures of the nationstate. To understand identify formation in terms of re-territorialization demands that we understand the art form of gardening as creating spaces from which place can be recuperated. This process took on added meaning for persons undergoing forced removal and multiple losses, with an art form such as gardening enacting a portable sense of place that helped internees re-root themselves in brutal and especially hostile physical settings. To survive in these locations of imprisonment, internees had few options but to *replace* what they had lost in terms of food, environmental aesthetics, and place.

CHAPTER 4

Making Connections

Many imprisoned Japanese Americans used art as a way of making and sustaining connections among themselves and with people outside the camps. Such a framework complicates the idea of community, which is often rooted in creating structures of sameness, homogeneity, and exclusionary thought. Although the idea of community sometimes allows us to freeze and study moments of cultural and social solidarity, we are often left with a utopian understanding that fails to encompass the complexity or full range of human experience. The idea of connections is offered as a tool for understanding how people relate with each other in more fluid ways that run along a continuum from momentary to long-lived alliances. Rather than emphasizing uniformity in values and ideas, this framework offers a way to highlight difference among people who choose to create bonds with one another. Here I offer connections as a way of thinking about the countless, complex, and imbricated practices that aid relational understandings among people while encompassing conflict and differences. Revealing these layered webs of everyday connections balances exclusionary understandings of community building and identity formation based on oppositional constructs of us versus them, with alternative forms of identification that may lead us to expand liberative social change. In this way, art created and sustained a myriad of intricate and layered connections among imprisoned Japanese Americans and friends beyond the confines of the barbed-wired camps. Art provided some internees with cultural practices that created connections based on identifying with each other rather than being identical to one another.[1]

The making of crafts sustained and reformed relationships among family members imprisoned together, with these activities often taking on gendered meanings in terms of art-making materials. Fathers and sons most commonly created art for family members with wood, whereas mothers and daughters employed yarn and fabric. Many art forms exchanged between family members addressed functional needs, as in the case of a chair made by Tom Kikuchi for his Issei father. The elder Kikuchi, a barber in Vallejo, California, before internment, brought his clippers with him to Tanforan, but he found cutting the hair of internee customers a cumbersome process because he had no barber's chair in which to seat them. By May 7, 1942, a short week after being transported to Tanforan, Kikuchi's three clippers were hanging on a wall in the family's living quarters next to a new barber's chair made by his son from a discarded barrel. Dramatic changes in social relations among family members had occurred, however. Charles, the eldest Kikuchi son, noted a change in his father's attitude after the first few days using his camp-made chair: "It's a bit pathetic when he so tenderly cleans off the clippers after using them; oiling, brushing, and wrapping them up so carefully. He probably realizes that he no longer controls the family group."[2]

Some fathers carved model boats for young sons and then accompanied the youngsters to camp-made ponds to launch their creations.[3] Most boats were carved from wood, but when supplies ran low, soap was substituted. Many of these boats were powered by wind, but some fathers searched the motor pool for discarded parts and equipped their sons' boats with engines. Other fathers constructed outdoor play equipment for their children. Hobbyhorses made from recently felled trees were especially popular among children at Rohwer, and youngsters imprisoned at Tule Lake spent many enjoyable hours in camp-made wooden carts.[4] Creating specialized outdoor chairs with "post-like prongs" that were pounded into the ground was also an art form favored by young men.[5] Making these portable seats took skill and practice, as evidenced by a teenager who worked for an entire evening before becoming so frustrated that he destroyed a chair he was making for his sister. Encouraged by family members to approach his project with more patience, the young crafter's subsequent attempt to build an outdoor chair proved successful.[6] Sometimes men crossed gender lines to create crafts for their mothers that were more commonly associated with the opposite sex. One young man imprisoned at Tanforan, especially skilled in the art of knitting, created a matching skirt and jacket for his mother. However, fear of being ridiculed prevented this talented crafter from knitting in public or displaying his work at exhibits.[7]

Mothers and daughters often worked together on knitting and sewing projects. With yarn received through the mail from a friend back home in San Diego, a mother imprisoned at Poston helped her fifth-grade daughter knit blankets and sweaters for her dolls. In a letter thanking her friend for the gift of yarn, the youngster wrote: "There is nothing I like better than to knit my head off."[8] A teenager imprisoned at Santa Anita knitted both her sister and brother-in-law a pair of socks for their first wedding anniversary, while her mother knitted a table runner to decorate the couple's living unit.[9] Women at Tanforan attended classes where they learned to make baglike containers to protect their eating utensils from dust as they carried them back and forth between their living quarters and the communal mess hall three times each day. Made with scrap pieces of cloth, the bags were often collaborative projects between mothers and daughters, who worked to create increasingly elaborate designs and then to translate them into patterns made from newspaper. After two months of sitting down to meals made less appetizing by dishes soiled with fine dust during long treks to the mess hall, a Nisei man was thankful for a protective bag sewn by his younger sister Emiko. After receiving this gift, he reported: "This is the latest fad. It is practical since it keeps our dishes from getting dusty."[10] Another Tanforan internee

30. Camp-made outdoor play equipment at Tule Lake, July 1, 1942. Photographer: Francis Stewart. Courtesy of the National Archives and Records Administration.

remembered these pieces of art as "ingenious containers" that grew more "elaborate in a sort of unspoken competition."[11]

Mothers maintained and strengthened relationships with family members by keeping them clothed in everyday fashions. Imprisoned at Topaz, Fumi Hayashi remembered her mother attending sewing classes and always finding time to make her daughter a new outfit for special occasions such as dances and parties. During an especially demanding pattern-drafting class, Hayashi's mother made her a tailored suit and coat, which her daughter continued to wear for ten years after being released from Topaz.[12] Another Topaz mother, who had been employed as a dressmaker in Oakland before the war, kept her daughter's wardrobe up to date by sewing pleated skirts. A woman friend in block 10 knitted "Sloppy Joe" sweaters to compliment the skirts. So, with her skirts reaching slightly below her knees and the long, oversized sweaters revealing only two or three inches of her skirt, Seiko Akahoshi was outfitted in the latest World War II–era fashion.[13]

Sewing machines were among the most difficult items for mothers to leave behind when the family was shipped to temporary imprisonment facilities. A bewildered fourteen-year-old girl from Oakland watched as her mother refused to board a bus destined for Tanforan because an armed military guard was unwilling to load her sewing machine. "I need it. I have eleven children," she replied to the guard who was ordering her to leave the machine behind. This Nisei mother stood her ground: "I'm sorry but I will not get on the bus without my machine." The mother blocked the bus door, and with a crowd gathering behind her, an officer standing nearby ordered the guard to load the machine.[14] Another girl, Katsumi Kunitsugu, remembered that once her family had been transported from Pomona to Heart Mountain, her mother immediately wrote friends back home in the downtown Los Angeles neighborhood of Boyle Heights and asked if they would retrieve her sewing machine from storage. When the machine arrived, Kunitsugu's mother set to making new clothes for her family of five. They were confined in a colder climate than the family was accustomed to, so winter clothes were her first priority.[15]

Sisters and daughters also recognized the importance of maintaining connections with family members by making garments, but more commonly they choose the art form of knitting to accomplish this goal. Imprisoned at Rohwer, a teenage girl from Stockton, California, was an accomplished knitter, but she reported that "I never cared much for sewing. My mother and older sister make most of my clothes and I just help with the little things [like] hooks, snaps, buttons, and the sort."[16] Preparing for cool winter evenings in the desert of Poston, Arizona, another teenager spent her late summer and early fall evenings knitting a sweater for her mother. Rusty brown in color with two cables running down the front, the sweater was finished by the beginning of October 1942, having taken four months to complete.[17] After enduring a cold Wyoming January with temperatures that frequently reached twenty below zero, a Heart Mountain teenage boy thankfully reported in a diary entry that his sister had finally finished knitting his sweater. Requiring five months of effort, Stanley Hyami's new sweater was certainly the work of a novice, but the crafter's experience was of little consequence. On the last Sunday of January 1943, Hayami wrote that receiving the sweater was a "memorable event" because of the warmth the gift provided."[18]

Women also aided their children and partners in creating and maintaining relationships by sewing costumes for performances, sporting activities, and other special occasions. Mothers, wives, and girlfriends of Tule Lake's baseball players made uniforms from mattress covers for the 1943 season, a year filled with highly spirited competitions. In the wake of the loyalty questionnaire debacle and designation of Tule Lake as a segregation center for "disloyal troublemakers" from other camps, sports enthusiasts imprisoned in this northern California concentration camp received an unexpected boost during the spring of 1943. Baseball devotees from other camps arrived with friendships and team allegiances already established, naming their new teams according to previous locations of imprisonment. Now expanded to eight full squads, Tule Lake's baseball league included teams from Gila, Topaz, Jerome, and Manzanar as well as four Tule Lake "home" teams. Women were not allowed to participate as players, but the uniforms they made were critical parts of a season that drew between 7,000 and 8,000 spectators for each game.[19] There is an inescapable irony here. The high levels of participation in and enthusiasm for baseball, a game thought of as an all-American sport, must have provoked remarks among some administrators in charge of a camp designated as a segregation center for internees who supposedly lacked appropriate levels of "loyalty" to the United States.[20]

Having taken ballet lessons in Oakland, California, before imprisonment, Dorothy Harada joined the Topaz high school "entertainment troupe," relying on her mother to make her costumes.[21] Always participating in school activities before imprisonment, another Oakland teenager transferred her enthusiasm to Topaz high school assembly programs, where she choreographed and performed jitterbug routines in sturdy garments created by her mother.[22] A Santa suit made by an Issei woman allowed connections between adults and children to be more easily enacted. As a Tule Lake block manager, Nobori Shirai was responsible for distributing several freight cars of toys sent by the Society of Friends to imprisoned children. At dusk on Christmas Eve 1943, Shirai donned the red cap and Santa suit sewn by his wife and spent the evening walking through thirteen barracks, ringing a bell and passing out gifts to exuberant children.[23] Although block managers were sometimes viewed as working too closely with camp administrators, Shirai likely found his reputation softened by his Christmas Eve appearance as Santa.

Employing camp-made art to re-form family connections was especially significant in the context of internment when we recall that dramatic changes occurred within the family, between husbands and wives, and children and parents. Fathers were displaced as primary breadwinners and authority figures, and supplanted by the U.S. government, which exercised control over the lives of these Japanese Americans. Many

31. Typical interior scene in one Manzanar barrack, June 30, 1942. Notice
the cloth partitions, which provide little privacy. Photographer Dorothea
Lange. Courtesy: National Archives and Records Administration.

fathers were separated from their families and imprisoned in facilities
run by the Department of Justice, the Federal Bureau of Prisons, or the
U.S. Army. The dynamics of intact family units were also restructured
by cramped and shoddily built living quarters. Because in some barracks
partitions reached only halfway to the ceiling, even quiet conversations
could be overheard, not to mention the typical arguments that all families experience. Even noises conveying the most intimate details of life
were shared by barrack mates. Spending extended periods of time inside

living quarters that were cramped, noisy, and lacked running water or plumbing was difficult for even close-knit families.

Traditional family structures were further degraded by the requirement that internees consume their meals in cafeteria-style mess halls designed to feed 3,000 people in ninety minutes.[24] Teenagers were soon taking their meals with friends as their parents sat across the mess hall. Young mothers often ate with their small children, while fathers gathered around tables where other men were seated. Mine Okubo reflected on the relationship between changing social relations and eating in communal messes when she recalled: "Table manners were forgotten. Guzzle, guzzle, guzzle; hurry, hurry, hurry. Family life was lacking. Everyone ate wherever he or she pleased. Mothers had lost control over their children."[25] Even if family members wanted to dine together, conflicting work schedules usually made this impossible. Enduring extremely low pay rates, male and female internees worked in the mess halls, camp medical facilities, and vegetable fields. Other internees were employed as fire safety and internal security officers, schoolteachers, camp newspaper reporters, and block captains. Because keeping the camps running at even subsistence levels meant working long and irregular hours, many internees found that coordinating a common eating time for their family was a low priority.

Art also aided in developing and maintaining relationships among friends imprisoned together. An internee who taught basic English evening classes at Topaz recalled an elderly male student giving her a lapel pin made by twisting blue crepe paper into a thread, which was then woven into a basket. Within the basket was an assortment of tiny shells carefully painted with nail polish and arranged to resemble a bouquet of flowers.[26] The arrangement featured lilies of the valley and was three inches long and two inches wide. Young men imprisoned at Manzanar made rings from discarded toothbrush handles and presented these works of art to girlfriends. When submerged in hot water, the handles became pliable and easily shaped into various sizes. Ring makers used nail polish remover to fuse the ends together, then sanded

32. Lapel pin made at Topaz. Photographer: Tobie Matava. Courtesy of the Topaz Museum.

off the rough edges. Small pieces of already-cut-up handles were carefully chosen by each artist on the basis of color and inlayed to form designs or initials.[27]

At Santa Anita, Fumiko Fukuyama employed art to identify with other internees by organizing her girlfriends to knit layettes and blankets for the 150 new mothers in camp. Working the midnight-to-morning shift as an admitting clerk at the hospital left her days "free" to supervise art activities among youngsters. In addition to teaching knitting to young girls, she had the task of locating yarn and needles, materials she solicited from friends outside the camp. Considering that her workdays were between twelve and fourteen hours long, Fukuyama's commitment to knitting was significant.[28] A group of Tanforan "jitterbug friends" displayed less dedication to the art form of embroidery, but they employed needlework to connect with one another. Learning to embroider so that they could emblazon the word *Tanforettes* on the upper-right side of their

newly purchased red jackets, these teenage girls accentuated their dancing skills by being clearly visible at social activities.[29]

Art activities made creating connections easier for some teenagers.
For the daughter of a celery farmer from Hayward, California, who
before internment counted animals as her best friends, portrait drawing evolved into an important connection-making exercise. Nobuko
Hanzawa's Rohwer living unit was a bustling center of crafting activity
as friends and acquaintances stopped by to have their portraits drawn
by this aspiring artist. Commenting on her newfound hobby, Hanzawa
wrote: "My teachers have told me that I have a great deal of talent in
art. I may not have talent but my ambition to draw is very great."[30] Boys
expressed their teenage crushes at Puyallup by carving the name of their
latest love interest on a slab of wood and then bravely delivering the
artwork in person. A more sophisticated suitor at Santa Anita created
a gardenia corsage from Kleenex tissues and lemon leaves for a girl he
was escorting to a graduation ball. Events celebrating the educational
accomplishments of recent high school graduates were common in all
temporary facilities, but they took on special significance given that
Japanese American teenagers had been prohibited from attending commencement exercises back home.[31]

Sewing became an especially appreciated connection-making exercise
when twenty-seven Jerome women responded to a desperate need for
clothing by offering their services altering and repairing clothes. Beginning in November 1942, internees were directed to bring their clothes to
Mrs. Alice Tsukimura at block 23, barrack 1, unit D. Although there was
no charge for the service, imprisoned Japanese Americans were instructed
to bring thread. During the first five days in operation, 117 items were
altered, and in December, when it became clear that more space was
required, an entire barrack was allotted to the enterprise.[32] Subsumed
under the auspices of Jerome's welfare office, the seamstresses received
wages from the War Relocation Authority, and with the added space they
expanded their services by offering to make new garments if internees

furnished material. By February 1943, the shop was so overrun with requests that a hold was placed on new orders so that clothing already on hand could be completed.[33] Tsukimura's shop remained busy, taking in 220 garments weekly in April 1943, when these artists also began sewing dish towels and aprons for mess hall workers, mailbags for internee mail deliverers, and smocks for barbers. Remarkably, many of these clothes were sewn by hand, and it was not until late May 1943 that camp administrators arranged for sewing machines to be placed in each block, with internee seamstresses instructing new crafters in the art of sewing.[34]

Internees imprisoned at all ten camps were issued military surplus clothing that dated from the First World War. Among these garments were peacoats, which camp crafters refashioned into stylish outer garments. A young girl imprisoned at Manzanar took her drab and oversized army coat to the alterations shop, where an elderly seamstress "tore the lining out, opened and flattened the sleeves, added a collar, put arm holes in," producing a "beautiful" cape. Other Manzanar seamstresses worked full time transforming old army clothes into thousands of shirts, slacks, and fashionable coats.[35] Taye Jow directed an especially welcomed art project by supervising a group of Manzanar sewers in the creation of fifty-dozen shower curtains, which were quickly installed in the communal bathing facilities.[36] A full three months after Manzanar opened, Japanese Americans incarcerated in this southeastern California camp were now able to bathe in privacy. These shower curtains were significant additions because lack of privacy was a common complaint among women, children, and men imprisoned in all ten camps.

Internees made small gifts that were easily mailed as a means of maintaining connections with friends imprisoned at other camps. On June 4, 1942, a Tulare family anxiously watched their eldest daughter, Sachi Egami, open a birthday package from her fiancé imprisoned at Manzanar. Inside was a tiny pair of intricately carved wood getas with straps made from a black-and-red-stripped necktie. Carefully etched on the polished wooden surface was her name, Sachiko.[37] Although Shiro

33. Picture of a dog drawn at Poston and mailed
on October 19, 1942. Courtesy of the Elizabeth Y.
Yamada Japanese American National Museum.

Nomura and his girlfriend were raised in the same Los Angeles neighborhood, they were imprisoned in Manzanar and Amache, respectively.
The separation and his feelings of loneliness were made more bearable
for Nomura by the arrival of a green hand-knitted sweater accompanied
by a brief note: "Finally finished your sweater. I hope it fits to keep you
warm till we're together. Love Amy." In spite of considerable ribbing
from his male friends, Nomura responded by learning the art of knitting
from his mother, and in a short time he created a "labor of love" in the
form of knitted woolen socks for Amy.[38]

34. Small items made with shells and wood were often given as gifts.
Photographer: Tobie Matava. Courtesy of the Heart Mountain, Wyoming,
Foundation.

Works of art were also used to make new connections outside the
barbed-wired confines of the camps. Young women imprisoned at
Jerome who were also YWCA members urged the national office to
connect them with groups that would find their "handicrafts useful."
In a letter to the Denver chapter, Mary Tsukamoto explained that her
female barrack mates were "clever with their hands" and that making
crafts for others would help "keep our minds strong and thoughts
alive with the outside." She solicitously continued: "If we could get
requests for little favors or nut cups or lapel pins, or even artificial
flowers, or anything like sewing, we would be happy to help out."[39]
An embroidery teacher organized an exhibit of his students' art at a
library in Powell, Wyoming, a town near Heart Mountain. A camp
newspaper article reported on January 9, 1943, that exhibiting 125
pieces of internee-made embroidery was a "first step toward establishing closer, friendlier relationships with those on the outside."[40] Here
we see imprisoned Japanese Americans constructing themselves as

more than internees by keeping their connections with the outside world alive and relevant.

Other small and easily packaged pieces of art were mailed back home, sustaining relationships with friends beyond camp boundaries. For many internees, these works of art thanked friends who mailed monthly boxes full of cookies, canned fruit, tea, crackers, candy, and rice. Imprisoned at Santa Anita, Roy Nakata and his family were the recipients of several care packages personally delivered by a friend. As a thank you, Nakata carved a pine knot in the shape of a heart and mailed the gift with a note that read: "We really do appreciate all your kindness from the bottoms of our hearts."[41] Gardenias and Easter lilies were likewise mailed by a Tule Lake woman to Jessie Treat in Palo Alto, California, as a token of gratitude for sending a long list of items, including a tea kettle, yarn, soap, and scotch tape. In a separate package were "corsages" made with shells collected from the ancient lake bed once located at the site of the camp. Gathering these shells was an especially perilous activity because women often encountered scorpions while sifting through the sand for these crafting materials.[42] A high schooler imprisoned first at Santa Anita and later at Poston received many care packages from Clara Breed, who was the children's librarian at the San Diego Public Library. In return, the teenage girl mailed a stream of thank you letters that often included artwork by her younger sister Florence. From Santa Anita, Margaret Ishino wrote: "Here is a house Florence drew for you. She hopes you like it!"[43] On October 19, 1942, Ishino included another drawing created by her sister and accompanied by this description: "Florence drew a picture of a dog at school she would like you to have."[44] Sending art through the mail was a common practice among artists of all ages as a way to retain connections with friends from pre–internment camp days who continued to enjoy their freedom.

Many internees sustained and created new bonds among themselves by exhibiting their artwork. Serving as webs of collectivities, the exhibits demonstrated the diversity of art created by imprisoned Japanese Americans. In these display spaces, internees gathered to participate in

35. Small objects were easily mailed to friends beyond the camp boundaries. Photographer: Tobie Matava. Courtesy of the Topaz Museum.

complicated, colorful, and rich visual conversations that revealed inhuman treatment, economic exploitation, and the dislocations encompassed by Executive Order 9066. Displaying a wide range of interests, form, materials, and style, these works of art provoked ideas, resistive practices, and strategies for improving both physical and mental conditions. Here, internees connected and formed attachments with the purpose of improving their lot in life. Embedded in these artifacts were subversions, with internees speaking about the control exerted on their lives. For people confined in barren and monochromatic environments, art shows also offered counter-landscapes, adding vibrancy and color to camp palates dominated by shades of tan.

Exhibits were frequent and varied in size, location, duration, and art form. Some small ones featured the work of a single class or block.

36. Attending exhibits was a popular activity in most camps. Amache, March 6, 1943. Photographer: Pat Coffey. Courtesy of the National Archives and Records Administration.

At Poston III, better known as Toaston to internees, female students in Mrs. Nakadate's knitting class organized a one-day exhibit in hall 318.[45] One of Manzanar's carpentry classes was more ambitious. The members held their first exhibit, which featured bookshelves, tables, chests of drawers, cupboards, bureaus, benches, and medicine cabinets with mirrors, at block 27, barrack 15, on January 9–11, 1943. The camp newspaper informed readers that pieces of furniture would be for sale and that the

37. Wood carvings made by students participating in the adult education classes at Amache, March 6, 1943. Photographer: Pat Coffey. Courtesy of the National Archives and Records Administration.

money raised would pay for new lumber and tools. Prospective buyers were assured of good deals when the reporter noted that labor fees were not included in the sale prices.[46] A class of Amache paper flower crafters was pleasantly surprised when three hundred internees turned out for an exhibit on a cold snowy day on the Colorado plains.[47] Cold weather was not a concern for Shigee Honma's Heart Mountain pupils, who organized a summer exhibit of their flower arrangements. The exhibit was held in a small room, at block 17, barrack 25, unit S, during June 18–20, 1943.[48] Similar works of art were displayed a month earlier in Jerome's hall 17, when Masao Hatano's ikebana students organized a small exhibit.[49]

Kobu was an art form commonly practiced in the Arkansas camps, with exhibits often featuring the work of internees living in a single block. Mess halls were favored as spaces for these block-centered art

38. Kobu used as a vase. Courtesy of the Estelle Ishigo
Papers, Department of Special Collections, Charles E.
Young Research Library, UCLA.

shows because of their high level of foot traffic. Artists of Jerome's block
42 spent much of their first January of imprisonment searching the local
Arkansas woods for kobu materials, in preparation for an upcoming
exhibit. The time and energy devoted to these searches were rewarded,
as evidenced by a rare and unusual spiral form further distinguished by
poison ivy entwined around a hickory root. Drawing internees to this art
form were the texture and color variations found in wood of the Arkansas
Delta area, which ranged from the smooth whiteness of persimmon roots
and multicolored oak tree roots to rough, wavelike, and banded patterns
of elm. Working with these varied materials, block 42 artists created and
exhibited pin cushion stands, toothpick holders, ashtrays, and plaques.[50]
Vases for flower arrangements were also favorite objects created by kobu
or tree-root artists.

These artists found as much enjoyment in searching the dense Arkansas woodlands for unique kobu material as they did in creating the final product. But the pleasures of exploring the 10,000 acres designated as the "camp reserve" were tempered by the knowledge that locals held Japanese Americans in contempt. These brewing animosities materialized just over a month after the camp opened when a farmer on horseback shot two internees. On a deer-hunting trip and armed with a shotgun, this local man came upon three internees chopping down trees for firewood as part of a "supervised work detail." Although a Caucasian War Relocation Authority engineer was with the internees at the time of the shooting, the farmer claimed that the internees were attempting to escape. No charges were filed against the trigger-happy hunter.[51]

Kobu artists imprisoned in block 31 at Jerome used their mess hall as a display space for an exhibit that opened on February 22, 1943, and continued for a full two weeks. It featured both natural formations found in the roots of trees and art carved from pieces of tree trunks. Among the natural shapes highly polished by internees were dancing couples, a monkey climbing a tree, a hunched cat, lizards, snakes, a seal's head, and cowboys. The carved shapes included plaques, candy bowls, trays, ashtrays, match holders, cigarette boxes, and sculptures featuring human images. As a special opening night celebration, block 31 invited block 43 to a talent show.[52] Reporting on the kobu displayed in this exhibit, the camp newspaper observed: "As a form of creative work it has been a boom to residents in improving their mental attitude."[53] Perhaps the smallest of all shows at Jerome was an exhibit featuring kobu created by a single artist. Seeming to have grown weary of the overwhelming productivity of tree-root crafters, the *Denson Tribune*, in its issue of March 16, 1943, announced a weeklong exhibit of Kamayashi Fuhara's creations with the headline "Another Kobu Show Opens." Fuhara predictably identified the mess hall serving his block 2 as the appropriate place for his solo exhibition.[54]

Jerome crafters also used their mess halls to display a wider range of art, with block 44 featuring artificial flowers, paintings, wood carvings,

39. Kobu artists at Rohwer and Jerome frequently
displayed their works. Courtesy of the Life
Interrupted Collection/University of Arkansas Little
Rock Archives and Special Collections.

and Densonware made from Jerome mud by the camp optometrist Dr.
Joseph Sasaki.[55] Perhaps also weary of viewing kobu, another group of
Jerome internees organized an exhibit without a single piece of tree-root
art. Instead, three life-sized busts made from plaster and cement were
featured, along with crepe-paper flower arrangements, miniature rock
gardens, needlecraft, oil paintings, and bookends created by Pat Shinno,
or what the camp newspaper referred to as "an example of feminine talent in wood carving."[56] Two blocks sponsored art shows in their mess
halls during March and April 1943, with block 46 including ikebana,
artificial flowers, needlecraft, and an assortment of children's work,
and of course the ever-present kobu.[57] Block 19 featured a special item,

with word quickly spreading throughout camp about a tiny inch-long violin accompanied by a case and bow. An interview with the artist, Ichiro Kitamura, revealed that this intricate piece of art had required a month of devoted effort. Spectators also had the opportunity to inspect elaborately constructed and polished dressers as well as candy dishes, ashtrays, and nut containers made solely from kobu found in the woods. Indicating that the exhibit would be of special interest to kobu purists, the newspaper noted that "none of the kobu has been patched." Paintings by Eizo Nakagawa depicting camp life were also crowd pleasers. During the first three days of the show, 3,500 internees attended.[58]

Many shows were sponsored by camp-organized art clubs, with classes joining together to exhibit works that appealed to a wide audience especially in terms of sexual difference and age. This collaborative strategy of attracting big crowds by exhibiting diverse art forms was successful, as a Heart Mountain exhibit in December 1942 illustrated. Sponsored by the Art Students League, the exhibit combined the work of Yeneji Morita's woodcraft class and Mrs. Kimi Ito's crocheting students, along with stone art, flower arranging, and paintings. An especially talented eight-year-old art student, Reiko Nagumo, displayed a group of his watercolors. Originally scheduled over a weekend, the show was extended until Monday night to accommodate the larger-than-expected crowds, which reached 3,000 by Sunday. Organizers wisely held the exhibit in a barrack that internees converted into a "recreation hall," which allowed viewers to more easily inspect especially popular items. Artwork documenting everyday camp life and made with materials found at Heart Mountain aroused the most interest. Internees lingered around a collection of polished stones painted with designs and figures, and a piece titled *Early Spring*, which was a blooming potted dwarf plum tree remarkably made by combining sagebrush, rice, and eggs.[59]

Students of Manzanar's Art Center and Art Institute held weeklong open houses beginning August 15, 1942. Both of these block-based organizations conducted classes in a wide variety of media, ranging from what most understand as fine art to crafts. Drawings, paintings, and sketches, along with woodcrafts and artificial flowers, were exhibited by both groups, with students from block 14's Art Center creating portraits for internees willing to take the time to pose.[60] Exhibits devoted to art created by children and teenagers were always well attended. Jerome's junior and senior high school students joined together to display bookshelves, bookends, desks, and more than seventy-five cedar chests and cabinets, along with final projects from costume design and painting classes. This art show drew a crowd of more than 2,000.[61] Another art exhibit, this one of summer session students at Heart Mountain, was held in the barracks housing the high school and attended by 2,000 internees. Especially large crowds gathered in front of a display featuring furniture made by children ranging from seven to twelve years of age.[62]

Manzanar internees living in four barracks, located in four separate blocks, shared exhibit space during the week of August 26, 1942. Without the use of carving tools or saws, Duke Tedera created a "perfect" replica of a Terminal Island fishing boat, which he attached to a wooden panel so the design could be hung on the wall. Japanese Americans living on Terminal Island were the first to be forcibly removed from their homes, even before the government opened temporary imprisonment facilities. Located in San Pedro Bay twenty-five miles south of Los Angeles, Terminal Island was a mere three and one-half miles long east to west and three-quarters of a mile wide north to south. At the turn of the twentieth century, Issei fishermen began settling on the island, marking the initial development of a racialized enclave, with people of Japanese ancestry occupying the southeastern portion of the island known as Fish Harbor and whites living in the midsection.

Most of Terminal Island's Japanese American population came from the Wakayama prefecture on the Kii peninsula in southwest Japan, which borders the Pacific Ocean and contains 600 kilometers of coastline. In America, these men worked on boats, some as captains of their own ships. Women were land bound and labored in cannery factories processing and packing fish caught by their brothers, husbands, and fathers. Fish Harbor was the home of 3,000 Japanese Americans, all of whom resided in company-owned housing. On February 9, 1942, Issei with commercial fishing licenses were rounded up by the FBI and incarcerated in Department of Justice facilities. Just over two weeks later, the remaining population was given forty-eight hours to pack up their lives and leave the island, with no alternative housing offered by the government. After their release from concentration camps, many Terminal Island internees settled in Seabrook, New Jersey, where they grew and packed vegetables for the Seabrook Company.

Campwide shows were the most common form of art exhibit. Tulare internees passed their first Fourth of July of imprisonment by organizing a festival that included an ambitious campwide craft show, which filled several large rooms. Getas, wood carvings, polished stones, and suzuris or ink wells used when creating calligraphy were displayed in one room, while knitted garments, embroidery, crocheting, and appliqué were grouped together. Another room was devoted exclusively to sewing. Knitted blankets, crocheted table scarves, and screens made by piecing together tiny scraps of wood were one Issei woman's favorites, but she admitted in her July 4, 1942, diary entry that the size of the exhibit prevented her from viewing all of the displayed artwork.[63] Santa Anita opened its two-day Fourth of July "gala" with an art show. According to the camp newspaper, the art displayed at the festival "was amazing in scope." Overwhelmed by the sheer volume of artwork, organizers found they had to set up the exhibit in two spaces. Among the items internees found at one location were a carved bust of Gen. Douglas MacArthur, lithographs of a cat, and a miniature reproduction of the camp, complete with grandstand, mess halls, and barracks, made out of paper by kindergarten students. Especially large crowds gathered around a "drawing class in action," where live models posed for students. A miniature garden, wood carvings, a wide assortment of furniture

40. A wide range of art was exhibited at camp shows, Amache, March 6, 1943. Photographer: Pat Coffey. Courtesy of the National Archives and Records Administration.

including Ken Matsumoto's chest of drawers made from cardboard and wallpaper, and tiny, decorative getas were available for inspection at the second display site.[64]

Organizers of the Anita Funita art show were experienced in staging such an event, having successfully hosted several other campwide exhibits in the short three months since the camp opened. On the first day of their June show, over 3,000 internees showed up to examine a wide range of art. The most unusual forms included boats carved from bars of soap, wastebaskets created with discarded newspapers, tiny wooden models of jeeps, and wallets, moccasins, and belts made from leather. A varied assortment of outdoor chairs made with rough tree branches illustrated efforts by newly imprisoned Japanese Americans to expand their living space beyond the cramped, noisy confines of their living quarters. An extensive needlecraft display featured not only the typical "feminine handicrafts" of knitted sweaters and crocheted doilies but also a handbag and a pair of socks knitted by a member of the boys' club.[65] Held in what the *Santa Anita Pacemaker* referred to as Handicraft Haven, located at barracks 36 and 37, this successful show also contained the usual model planes, bird lapel pins, decorative wooden panels, paintings, drawings, and carved wooden sculptures.[66]

A five-day arts and crafts exhibit held during the first spring of imprisonment at Manzanar featured "floral designs" created by internees living in blocks 14 and 18, needlework created by a class of block 4 crafters, as well as carved wooden figurines and copper work from across the entire camp.[67] By December 1942, a Visual Education Museum located at block 8, barrack 15, was established by internees, where they held a holiday craft and art show. Hosting overflow crowds of 2,000 internees each day, organizers extended the show, keeping the doors open between Sunday, December 20, and Saturday, December 26. Among the most popular art forms were carved wooden canes, vases and lamps made from ice cream and popsicle sticks, stone and shell art, model ships of "every description," posters made to "adorn" the walls of living units, and cabinets of "excellent design." Especially large crowds gathered around exhibits of internee-made toys, children's drawings, and a lathe made entirely from scrap iron found on the grounds of the camp.[68]

Once the holiday exhibit closed, crafting enthusiasts immediately began work on another campwide show scheduled to open January 11. Although all art forms were welcomed, this show was centered around wood carvings from pear, apple, and plum trees and needlework, especially embroidery, knitting, and crocheting. No longer limiting internees to exhibiting three items at any one show, organizers asked that all works of art be delivered to the museum by noon on Saturday, January 9, to allow plenty of time to design and set up the display space.[69] Art exhibits continued to rotate through Manzanar's Visual Education Museum, with yet another show beginning Saturday, January 23. This

41. Much needlework featured floral designs.
Photographer: Tobie Matava. Courtesy of the Heart
Mountain, Wyoming, Foundation.

show featured mainly paintings and drawings by both children and
adults, but the camp newspaper noted that the display of carved wooden
figurines and jewelry was drawing huge groups of girls. A crouched pan-
ther brooch "distinctively painted and varnished" appeared to be particularly appealing, with many passersby noting the artist's name.[70] On
February 3, the *Manzanar Free Press* announced the fourth show at the
museum in less than two months and informed readers that chopsticks,
getas, and slippers would be the focus, with all valuable items placed in
a glass case for protection.[71]

Campwide exhibits were record breakers, attracting huge crowds. An
exhibit held in the high school auditorium at Poston drew 11,000 internees from all three units over a May weekend in 1944. Knitted garments,
shodo (calligraphy), a model train made by the toy department, and a
wedding gown made by block 21's sewing school were among the crafts

produced primarily from scrap and waste materials. As sponsors of the exhibit, the Community Activities Committee requested that the clearly devoted crowd cooperate in making the show a success by "keeping their hands off" displayed artwork.[72] Jerome also held campwide shows featuring the ubiquitous kobu. A total of 7,000 internees turned out for a weeklong exhibit organized for April 1943 and were allowed to vote on their favorite works of art. A miniature chest made by Eidi Takesako won the grand prize, Kamaemon Tahara's cow placed second, and a flower vase by Yeisaku Fujimani came in third. All three artists received cash prizes ranging from five to ten dollars.[73]

Another campwide exhibit that drew record-breaking crowds was directly linked to gender. Jerome's Fujin Kai (mothers' club) organized a "women's handicraft exhibit" over Mother's Day weekend. Women crafters were instructed to bring their works of art to any of Jerome's mess halls by Thursday, when a truck was scheduled to make the rounds and pick up the items. Internees with fragile pieces were advised to personally deliver their creations to mess hall 17, the location of the art show. An especially diverse collection of artifacts, the exhibit included knitting, embroidery, sewing, crocheting, quilting, carvings of wooden figures and panels, weaving, kobu, painting, drawing, flower arranging, carved and painted gourds, and flowers made with crepe paper and Kleenex tissues. Originally scheduled for a three-day run, the show was extended through Wednesday to accommodate overflow crowds. In a special celebration of Mother's Day, a Sunday crowd of nearly 3,000 set Jerome's single-day attendance record for art shows.[74]

Several well-known artists, including Chiura Obata, Mine Okubo, and Matsusaburo and Haruko Hibi, were imprisoned at Tanforan, so it was an especially active site for artistic production and campwide craft shows. A crowd of 9,000 internees surprised organizers of a campwide show held between July 11 and 14 because only 8,000 persons were imprisoned at Tanforan. Future exhibits were planned with the knowledge that many internees would make multiple visits to the same art show. Novice artists exhibited a wide range of objects, including hats woven from tule grasses gathered within the barbed-wire perimeters of the camp; vases, ashtrays, and furniture created out of eucalyptus tree roots found in Tanforan's dump; woodcrafts carved from discarded racetrack fence posts; and lamps made with auto parts scavenged in the motor pool. Internee crafters also displayed bookends, getas, needlework, leather crafts, braided work, paintings, drawings, and model airplanes. Also, with Tanforan having two ponds, it is not surprising that exhibits there featured as many as six hundred model boats on a single day. Artistic output reached such high levels that separate exhibits were organized to accommodate flower and vegetable arrangements. Apparently the manure-rich surroundings of this former racetrack provided especially fertile soil for gardeners, who planted flowers and vegetables by their living units, which previously had stabled horses. Flower shows were often held at the site of a community garden, with each attendee receiving a bouquet arranged by internee artists.[75]

Classes of course were more monolithic in size and duration than exhibits, but just as varied in terms of art form, training of the teachers, and skill of the students. Like exhibits, classes created connections between persons of diverse backgrounds and interests, serving as webs of collectivities where internees developed new attachments and created art that sustained already established relationships. Attempts by internees to organize classes were not always welcomed by camp officials. A group of Japanese Americans imprisoned at Heart Mountain submitted a petition to the camp director requesting permission to form an Art Students League. Arguing that art was neither "a necessity or necessarily a public interest," War Relocation Authority officials initially denied this request, but after continued pressure, officials granted internees the temporary use of one-half of a barrack, with the stipulation that all classes be "educational." Heart Mountain's crafters struggled for nearly a year, hoping to secure a permanent site for their activities. Only after agreeing to produce 4,000 silk-screened posters for the U.S. Navy did the

42. Heart Mountain art class, January 11, 1943. Photographer: Tom Parker. Courtesy of the National Archives and Records Administration.

Art Students League gain legitimacy in the eyes of camp administers and a permanent space for art classes.[76] A letter addressed to camp administrator Guy Robertson from U.S. Navy Captain Fink expressed appreciation to the War Relocation Authority for completing a "rush" job on the government posters.[77] Kasen Noda, an Issei man imprisoned at Poston, experienced similar obstacles when he was approached by members of the women's club in his block about teaching calligraphy classes. Plans were halted when a camp administrator informed the group that they must first seek permission.[78]

Many Heart Mountain internees ignored the reluctance of camp administrators to support art activities by organizing their own informal classes. Only fifteen days after opening, more than 200 girls and women were participating in flower-arranging classes taught by Mary Shigeo Homma. Morning and afternoon classes were the most popular, but the

Heart Mountain Sentinel informed internees on waiting lists that evening classes were planned for the future.[79] Heart Mountain internees interested in learning to make artificial flowers from cloth began meeting on September 14. By late September, Rosa Sato and Masako Sugihara were teaching fashion illustration and dress design from nine in the morning until four in the afternoon, six days a week, with Sunday their only day off.[80] Although admitting that there were severe shortages of materials and tools, Ben Torigumi continued organizing classes for model airplane, boat, and train builders, as well as for wood and linoleum carvers. Meeting each day between nine and five, students were crowded into a small room but were fortunate to have an aeronautical engineer and an industrial design specialist among their volunteer teachers. Youngsters over the age of ten were especially urged to enroll in classes organized by Torigumi.[81]

Although plans for a ceramics factory at Heart Mountain never materialized, internees harnessed equipment and training provided by the U.S. government to establish a small pottery center where classes were offered. Originally conceived of by War Relocation Authority officials as a means of producing tableware for the armed forces and all ten concentration camps, the factory was to have a labor force of one hundred internees and mass-produce 6,000 pieces of tableware weekly. Efforts to train workers began in late September 1942, when a ceramics specialist visited the camp. Motorized pottery wheels and electric kilns were later shipped to an administrative garage, where a small group of internees learned to make clay, glazes, and molds and became skilled at creating vessels on the wheels. Minnie Negoro, an art student at the University of California, Los Angeles, before internment, became an accomplished potter while in the camp, whereas Clem Oyama applied his pre-internment work experience as a chemist in his father's Los Angeles cosmetic plant to Heart Mountain's ceramics project. As an expert analyzer of mud, Oyama was responsible for determining which mixtures of clay contained appropriate levels of both elasticity for shaping and density for withstanding kiln temperatures that reached 2,500 degrees. Allowed to search within a sixty-mile radius of the camp, internees hit pay dirt when they located an extensive deposit of pottery-making clay at the site of a canal project three miles north of Cody, Wyoming.

In late May 1943, the *Heart Mountain Sentinel* announced that War Relocation Authority plans for a thousand-square-foot factory were suddenly being abandoned. Although circumstances surrounding this "change in policy" remain unclear, we can only hope that government officials came to their senses and were troubled by the thought of exploiting the labor of unjustly imprisoned people. Perhaps this explanation is excessively optimistic, but regardless of the government's motivations, imprisoned Japanese Americans found valuable art-making resources at their disposal. Instead of working in an industrial setting, Heart Mountain's crafters began taking classes from teachers trained at the expense of the government. In less than eight months, internees mined and transformed over a thousand pounds of mud into clay from which a wide range of forms were created. Having weathered high temperatures in the kiln, camp-made teapots, bowls, and cups were ideal for making snacks and hot drinks on potbellied stoves and hotplates located in living quarters. These works of art allowed the prohibition against cooking in living quarters to be defied, with some internees appreciating the privacy afforded by eating alone and others inviting friends over to share simple meals. Small figurines and decorative vases were also produced, along with especially popular ashtrays. Located in the south wing of block 16's community activities barrack, the flourishing pottery school also served as the site of high school arts and craft classes.[82]

Some art classes were taught by professional artists. Three days after arriving at Tanforan, Chiura Obata, a professor of art at the University of California, Berkeley, approached administrators hoping to obtain space for an art school. Although camp officials were initially hesitant to grant such a request, coaxing on the part of internees was successful, and the Tanforan Art School opened on May 25 in what had formerly been mess hall 6. Supplies were provided by friends, students from the university, and the American Friends Service Committee. With Obata as its director, the Tanforan Art School was open daily from nine in the morning until seven in the evening, offering classes in figure drawing, composition, still life, pencil drawing, landscape, sculpting, cartoon drawing, commercial art, fashion design, interior decorating, and brushwork. Many of the sixteen teachers were professionally trained artists who were well equipped to teach elementary, high school, and college students as well as the general adult population of the camp. Nearly all of the students enrolled in classes had little previous experience creating art. In the opening week of operation, the art school was a thriving center of artistic expression boasting 300 students.[83]

Santa Anita's art activities were supervised by Bob Kuwahara, who before December 7, 1941, had worked in the animation departments of Disney and MGM studios. Trained at the Otis Art Institute in Los Angeles, now known as the Otis College of Art and Design, Kuwahara was one of the primary artists contributing to the production of the movies *Snow White* and *Bambi*. Teaching classes of his own on Mondays and Wednesdays at barrack 36-E, better known as Handicraft Haven to internees, this Nisei artist was a populist when it came to artistic expression. Commenting on the opening of the art school in early June 1942, Kuwahara explained: "Art is not only cultural, but practical as well. It is a natural part of our existence."[84] Part of his job was allocating adequate space and time to competing art forms. Once demand outstripped these resources, organizers likely expected tensions between crafters to follow.

In July, Mrs. Sumi Kashiwagi, a needlecraft teacher, was busy assuaging the worries of 175 women knitters and crocheters concerned that the increasing interest in sewing would cause their classes to be discontinued. Instead, Santa Anita's art center decided to offer beginning sewing classes for over one hundred internees on a waiting list and to postpone advanced classes for over 450 students graduating from a two-month class covering the basics of sewing. Anxieties among knitters were likely rooted in an earlier May meeting at which 250 women needleworkers voted to establish the most popular art form and thereby garner the majority of resources. Knitters outnumbered sewers, with crocheting coming in third and pattern drafting placing fourth. Just over two months later, this hierarchy was reversed, with sewing replacing knitting as the most practiced needlecraft.[85]

Novices joined professionally trained artists in teaching a wide range of crafting classes. At Jerome, Mary Tsukamoto was surprised to see a friend teaching women the art of artificial flower making. "All I knew was that she was a strawberry grower's wife and I knew she could pick strawberries. Here she was a teacher of this crepe-paper flower making class."[86] Many art forms were developed in specific camps, spontaneously producing teachers who were inexperienced artists before imprisonment. Tule Lake and Topaz women were the most common practitioners of shell art, creating lapel pins, earrings, brooches, and artificial flowers from tiny shells, some as small as a grain of rice. An Issei woman imprisoned at Tule Lake explained in a letter to a friend that she had to dig five or six feet into the ground to find acceptable specimens. Teachers of this art form were active experimenters, developing techniques on the spot that included bleaching the shells and coloring the creations with fingernail polish. Japanese Americans imprisoned at Rohwer created jewelry by flattening pieces of tin cans salvaged from mess hall trash cans. Innovators of this art form taught other internees to stencil the metal with carpenters' nails and further shape the material into bracelets and rings.[87]

Beginning in June 1942 and under the supervision of internees, a wide variety of classes got under way at Manzanar, with two barracks reserved for painting, sketching, lettering, poster designing, and fashion drawing and another two barracks reserved for crafts made with wood, metal, leather, and linoleum. An additional woodcraft center for children was planned to open in the coming month.[88] Needlecraft and flower-arranging classes were gender specific, with the camp newspaper informing

43. Jewelry created from discarded tin cans at Rohwer. Courtesy of the Rosalie Santine Gould Collection.

internees that sessions for men and boys were a "no women's land." "There," the reporter continued, "the stalwarts are taught the womanly arts of knitting, sewing, crocheting, embroidery and flower making." If the class schedule was any indication, the "men only" classes were a big hit. Needlework classes were offered on Monday and Friday evenings and again on Saturday afternoons. Flower making was scheduled for three hours on Friday evenings and four hours each Saturday afternoon.

Although needlecraft and flower-making classes for men were confined to evening and weekend hours, women were able to choose from a wider selection of times. The efforts of Yumi Ogura and Linda Kinoshita, who offered sewing classes every day and evening except Sunday, were matched by Katsuko Asaka's commitment to teaching artificial flower making every day and for two hours on Tuesday and Thursday evenings. Women laboring at camp jobs were the focus for Mary Tamaki, who accommodated work schedules by offering classes exclusively in the evenings between six and nine. Rather than teaching women how to create decorative items, Tamaki's specialty was more practical, with students learning to create socks, sweaters, caps, mittens, and gloves. Women getting off work were encouraged by the *Manzanar*

Free Press to "dash over" to block 16, barrack 15, for an evening of productive crafting.[89] These classes were added to those offered since June 6 at 16–15's art center. At this location Takeo Itokawa supervised lettering, sketching, and painting classes, while Grace Ito was in charge of teaching needlework and flower making. Roy Satow had his hands full organizing the many woodcraft sessions.[90]

As the experiences of imprisoned Japanese Americans illustrate, art can be used to create a myriad of connections that enhance chances of survival. Through and with art, internees connected with each other in complicated and overlapping webs of connections embedded in the details of everyday life. By sewing clothes for one another, creating crafts as gifts, and participating in classes and exhibits, internees operated within these webs, which encompassed countless points and forms of connections. Although the idea of community often legitimizes existing social hierarchies and exclusionary ways of thinking that manufacture insiders and outsiders, connection is offered as a framework for identifying linkages between people in environments of difference and even dissent. These bonds maybe fluid, momentary, and unstable but no less powerful than identities grounded in the idea of community. In our search for community, we can blur everyday lived experiences in which people manage conflict and heterogeneity to create connections with one another. Ideas such as community can fabricate consensus and structure our thinking so we miss identifying moments of connections that are critical to surviving in oppressive environments such as those of the Japanese American concentration camps. Imprisoned Japanese Americans used art to create these connections and to identify with others within and outside the confines of barbed wire, an especially vital activity considering that heterogeneity among internees defined camp life.

Thinking about camp artists with the idea of connections rather than community can also help us understand how people create bonds when physically isolated from one another. Some camp crafts were made in the absence of others, an important experience to think about because it reveals that creating connections between people through art can be accomplished in solitude. An Issei women imprisoned at Tanforan and later Topaz preferred the art of knitting because she longed for "quiet moments to reflect." Although Iku Uchida enjoyed knitting because this activity allowed her to work alone, this act of crafting was part of a larger collaborative project. By knitting sweaters, Uchida was creating important connections with her daughters, who, in the context of internment, were especially grateful to their mother for devoting time to their wardrobe concerns.[91] Many other works of art were created in isolation and later given as gifts and exhibited at camp art shows. These crafting activities formed vital webs of connection and placed difference at the center of human experience. Thinking with the idea of connection can help us as we identify how people create linkages outside structures that legitimize hierarchies and at least partially escape a prevalent understanding of commonality as the sole foundation on which people create socially productive alliances. In environments of difference, Japanese Americans connected with each other through art to help negotiate and articulate their experiences as internees.

CHAPTER 5

Mental Landscapes
of Survival

Just as internees enhanced their chances of survival by employing art to create more livable physical places, they also linked crafting with solace to remake emotional, psychic, and mental landscapes of survival. For internees, art was a coping mechanism, and they combated depression by keeping their hands and minds busy. But imprisoned Japanese Americans also created an understanding of mental survival that joined aesthetic considerations with emotional well-being. Art activities served as spaces where personal visions of individual artists evolved into collective considerations and social life. With art, some internees articulated mental landscapes of survival for themselves and then offered these visions to other internees by participating in classes and shows, and by giving art as gifts. With classes, exhibits, and gifts, Japanese Americans created agency in their lives by participating in collective dialogues that revealed artful identifications between individuals and collectivities, the psychic and the material, art and politics, oppression and change. In this chapter I ask readers to think about camp-made material objects not as static reflectors or containers of the past but as items that enhanced psychic health even in environments where mental and emotional well-being were under constant assault. Art created spaces where ideas and strategies for survival could be revealed and refined. Here we can view internee-created art as both material and psychic practices of agency.

Imprisoned Japanese Americans were aware that unoccupied time posed threats to their emotional and mental health because these moments were too often filled with thoughts and feelings of despair, hopelessness, and intense anxiety. Feelings of personal psychological vulnerability were reinforced as internees witnessed friends and family members develop crippling mental illnesses.[1] At Santa Anita, Lillie McCabe's former dentist filled his days with endless walks around the guarded fence. Concerned about his declining physical and mental condition, McCabe advised her old friend to avoid getting "too caught up in this situation." But after months of continuously walking in circles, the dentist began hallucinating and eventually "lost his mind." Once McCabe was shipped to Amache, she followed her own advice, always "fighting to keep happy" rather than focusing on "morose" feelings.[2]

A young woman imprisoned at Stockton watched her older sister gradually slip into a severe depression, which intensified once they were shipped to Rohwer. Active and engaged before internment, Mary Sugitachi's sister arrived at Rohwer, after a long four-day train trip, with few psychic reserves and was soon unable to muster the energy or focus to cope with the many routine hardships of camp life. Long mess hall and latrine lines, combined with crowded and degraded living conditions, produced frequent anxiety attacks that made life even more difficult for Sugitachi's sister and those who cared for her.[3] A teenage girl became psychotic and was hospitalized soon after being transported to Puyallup. Interviewed for an "incident report," the teenager's friend frankly informed a camp administrator that although the girl had been a quiet person before imprisonment, "the events of evacuation were more than [her friend] could adjust to."[4] Depression was so common among internees that easily treated physical illnesses were often incorrectly diagnosed as "melancholia." Mabel Ota's father was sent to the Phoenix Sanitarium from Gila and died after six weeks of shock treatment intended to treat catatonic depression. Granted a travel permit because of her father's impending death, Ota arrived at the sanitarium and was informed by the attending physician that her father was not suffering from melancholia but from diabetes. Accepting the camp doctor's diagnosis, the psychiatrist proceeded with treatment and only conducted a thorough exam once Ota's father slipped into a fatal comma.[5]

For some Japanese Americans, the thought of internment drove them to consider suicide. Orphaned when she was in elementary school and with her older sister dead from tuberculosis just before imprisonment, fifteen-year-old Helen Murao assumed the position of authority for her family of three, which included herself and two younger brothers. Realizing she was about to be shipped off to the temporary center located near Portland, Oregon, Murao was overwhelmed by negative thoughts and a debilitating depression. "I really entertained, at fleeting moments, some feelings that maybe I'd be better off if, you know, I tried to, I felt it might be a solution if I just did away with my brothers and my own life."[6] Imprisoned at Minidoka, Hanaye Matsushita struggled with a similar depression and often found summoning the energy to write letters an impossible task. Explaining a recent dearth of letters, Matsushita wrote to her husband incarcerated at a Department of Justice facility in Fort Missoula, Montana: "I have many things to tell you, but in the afternoons I am worthless because of the horrible heat. When I dwell on the situation, I have suicidal feelings."[7]

For others these thoughts tragically came to fruition. Hideo Murata, an Issei from Pismo Beach, killed himself and was found holding a Certificate of Honorary Citizenship. Awarded to him at a Fourth of July celebration the previous year, the certificate read: "Monterey County presents this testimony of heartfelt gratitude, of honor and respect for your loyal and splendid service to the country in the Great World War. Our flag was assaulted and you gallantly took up its defense."[8] Although the focus of *Artifacts of Loss* remains on how internees managed to survive the brutalities encompassed by Executive Order 9066, it is critical to remember that many Japanese Americans did not emerge from this tragic experience emotionally, mentally, or physically intact. Even decades after

44. Some Japanese Americans were driven to suicide by their internment experience. Rohwer, January 1944. Courtesy of the National Archives and Records Administration.

being released, many former internees continue to bear emotional scars as well as physical problems caused by their imprisonment in concentration camps, where health care rarely reached minimal standards.

With everyday life providing convincing evidence that internment encompassed persistent and continuous assaults on mental health, many internees filled even limited moments of unoccupied time with activities that engaged their minds and bodies. Reacting to the traumas of imprisonment by doing anything less translated into long days that, in the words of one internee, "dragged endlessly."[9] Explaining the plethora of art activities organized by internees, a woman imprisoned first at Fresno and later at Jerome recalled that "we hastily tried to keep everybody busy."[10] In this context, "free" time became the enemy, with art serving as a powerful medium through which internees could at least partially focus on hope and new possibilities rather than on despair and anguish. Filling her first difficult days at Tanforan with furniture building, Mine Okubo recalled: "Many of the discomforts of the camp were forgotten in this activity."[11] Gladys Ishida Stone remembered her mother filling every spare moment at Amache by crocheting tablecloths and interpreted her mother's artful activities as doing "battle with the policy of internment and evacuation."[12] As the director of the Tanforan and later the Topaz art schools, Chiura Obata firmly believed in the power of art to raise the spirits of imprisoned Japanese Americans. Communicating the mission of the Tanforan Art School, Obata wrote that by creating art, "the general moral of the people will be uplifted."[13] For many internees creating, exhibiting, consuming, and thinking about art became embedded in the everyday patterns of camp life and helped ensure mental and emotional survival.[14]

Camp-made art helped internees reveal and cope with the many losses they were forced to endure, an important psychic exercise considering the scope and depth of despair that defined the implementation of Executive Order 9066.[15] Many art forms were used to express both temporary and permanent human losses. As young male internees traded imprisonment for service in a newly formed all-Nisei U.S. Army combat unit, Heart Mountain women and girls hurriedly sewed and embroidered one-thousand-stitch belts and vests or senninbari to protect their friends, husbands, sons, and brothers.[16] An art form based in Japanese culture, these "charmed" belts were made with long strips of white cloth and a single unbroken red thread knotted and stitched by one thousand women to represent their collective strength and power. Perhaps the most divisive and painful internment experiences for many imprisoned Japanese Americans, the decision by the U.S. War Department to recruit soldiers from the camps, provoked heated and frequent debates among internees throughout the winter and spring of 1943. Women sewing and embroidering senninbari at Heart Mountain likely encompassed special significance since only the Wyoming camp had an organized resistance movement— first referred to as the Heart Mountain Congress of American Citizens and

45. Senninbari vests were made to protect friends,
husbands, sons, and brothers who joined the U.S.
armed forces. Courtesy of the Japanese American
Archival Collection, Department of Special Collections
and University Archives, at the Library, California State
University, Sacramento.

later the Fair Play Committee. Senninbari served as important artifacts
of loss as Nisei males left their loved ones behind in the barbed-wire concentration camps to join the 442nd Regimental Combat Team and later to
fight and die on battlefields of France and Italy.

Insulting loyalty questionnaires were instituted by the U.S. government as a method for supposedly determining the "resettlement" suit-
ability of internees. More importantly, the questionnaires served as the
basis for registering all Nisei men of draft age. Questions 27 and 28 on

the government form asked if respondents were willing to serve in the U.S. armed forces and if they swore allegiance to the United States of America. Affirmative responses to both questions earned young men the "right" to fight and die for a country whose government continued to incarcerate their parents, wives, and siblings in concentration camps. As difficult as this decision was for many men, the possibility of serving as American soldiers was an attractive alternative to imprisonment. Joining the military also represented the ultimate expression of national allegiance, with many young men linking service in the U.S. armed forces with their hopes for a better future at the conclusion of the war. For a camp especially divided over the issue of sending young Nisei men to war, senninbari likely served as an important display of patriotism and support for Japanese American soldiers.

Imprisoned at Amache and worried about her two sons serving in the army, forty-six-year-old Kotono Kato purchased two pieces of silk and embroidered the image of a tiger on each. Symbols of strength and luck, tigers are described in a Japanese proverb as traveling one thousand miles but always safely returning to their homes. To achieve the perfect color, Kato dyed thread already on hand and purchased a black marble from a small boy to use as eyes. Assisted by her husband, who split the marble and made an embroidery frame from scraps of wood, Kato quickly completed the tigers and mailed them to her sons, Roy and Alfred. Despite a life marked by hardships that encompassed arriving in San Francisco at the age of eighteen as a picture bride, working as a farm laborer picking prunes, grapes, and apples, losing two of her six children, and being imprisoned at Merced and Amache, Kato would later understand her past as filled with good fortune because eventually Roy and Alfred returned safely to her. Instead of being shipped overseas, the boys uncharacteristically completed their tours on U.S. soil, never parting with their embroidered good luck charms. When last checked in 1989, Roy's and Alfred's wallets still contained the tigers made by their mother. Returning to California when released from Amache, Kato continued making art by creating new designs for knitting, crocheting, and embroidery projects.[17]

Jerome's Buddhist community also employed art as expressions of both the temporary and permanent loss of loved ones. Over five hundred miniature omyoge (Buddhist scrolls) were created by Denson's Young Buddhist Association and given to departing soldiers and the families they were leaving behind. Inserted into small cardboard carriers the size of a business card, these scrolls were inscribed with "Namu-amida butsu," a Buddhist expression of gratitude. These artifacts of loss were printed in beige and yellow with a template made from floor linoleum. Once the ink was dry, rayon covers were pasted over the thick cheviot paper to preserve these gifts of remembrance.[18] Creating less devout art was a high priority for an Issei mother imprisoned at Tule Lake, who often included knitted socks and artificial flowers in packages mailed to her soldier son.[19] These material objects of loss aided in creating new mental spaces in which unspeakable fear, worry, and despair were contained and navigated. Working together, these new landscapes of the mind and art aided internees in materializing and communicating their losses. Here, loss evolved into public sculptures rather than remaining solely the material of individual psyches left to ferment in isolation. In this way psyches were made more flexible, and they exhibited the ability to turn individual experiences of sorrow and emotional pain into collective life, an important step in expressing agency and power.

An especially touching use of artwork occurred when children's creations were mailed to their fathers imprisoned in Department of Justice facilities. Three-year-old Masahiro Iwata's art was often a topic of discussion in letters exchanged between his mother and father. Separated from his wife and three children, who were incarcerated at Poston, Shigezo Iwata was among thousands of Issei rounded up by the FBI in the aftermath of December 7, 1941. In a separate but parallel incarceration, these men and women were held in facilities controlled by the Justice Department. Imprisoned first at Sante Fe and later in Lordsburg, New Mexico, Shigezo

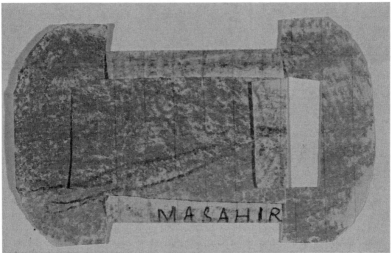

46. Masahiro's artwork was often mailed to his father, who was imprisoned in a Department of Justice facility. Courtesy of the Balch Collection, Historical Society of Pennsylvania Archives.

relied on his wife, Sonoko, to keep him informed about his children. On June 15, 1942, she wrote: "Every morning he comes home with something he has done at school and today he brought home a cut-out horse. Some are torn by the time he reaches home but I am enclosing two which I was able to save."[20] Agreeing with his mother's assessment of Masahiro as a prolific crafter, a teacher reported in 1944 that drawing remained a favorite activity of Masahiro's.[21]

Although the Student Relocation Program sponsored by the American Friends Service Committee provided imprisoned college-age Nisei with welcome opportunities for release, their experiences encompassed a strange, unsettling mix of relief, regret, and loss. Although young Japanese American men and women embraced the chance to earn a college education, they left family members behind in bleak environments where imagining hopeful futures was difficult at best. Providing money for visits was beyond the means of many parents, who struggled as truck farmers to makes ends meet before internment or lost accumulated wealth in the economically exploitive atmosphere created by Executive Order 9066. But making and selling art provided one Minidoka mother with the means to finance a reunion with her absent child. Tomae Tamaki earned her daughter Esther's train fare from St. Paul, Minnesota, to Minidoka by making "Indian moccasin pins" for a local man, who sold them at souvenir stands and state fairs. As a participant in the Student Relocation Program, Esther was released from Portland's temporary imprisonment facility on September 8, 1942, to attend Macalester College in Minnesota, while her mother, father, and two sisters were shipped to Minidoka. After nearly a year of creating one-inch moccasins out of tiny beads and chamois cloth, Tamaki saved enough money to purchase a round-trip ticket for her daughter. To add insult to injury, the War Relocation Authority demanded that Tamaki pay for her daughter's meals during the much-anticipated visit. Euphoric over being reunited with her family after a year's separation, Esther later remembered seven nights of sleeping on a straw-filled mattress in her family's cramped Minidoka living unit as the "best vacation of my life."[22]

Using art to materially memorialize permanent human losses was often an excruciating mental exercise for camp artists. An Issei woman who had learned to make paper flowers from her mother in Japan began teaching classes in this art form once she was imprisoned at Amache. Soon she was applying her skills to making funeral wreaths out of crepe-paper flowers for internees whose soldier sons who were killed in action. Although this task was emotionally wearing because it provoked disturbing thoughts about her own two sons serving in the army, this mother and artist fought back her fears to complete many funeral wreaths and provide solace for mourning parents. Wreaths made for dead soldiers usually included streamers made from red, white, and blue ribbons, which were attached to an eagle created by a camp wood-carver. Frames for the funereal wreaths were made with sagebrush collected on camp grounds.[23]

With over 700 Nisei soldiers killed in 225 days of combat, and over 2,000 wounded, religious leaders in all camps were busy as they prepared for funeral ceremonies and comforted relatives of wounded soldiers.[24] When Heart Mountain families received letters notifying them that their sons, husbands, and fathers had been killed in action, they placed gold star banners in barrack windows, with one internee commenting that Heart Mountain "started to look like Christmas time." These memorials where accompanied by funeral services, which included floral arrangements made from crepe paper by Buddhist women. Having attended many of these funerals, a nineteen-year-old Nisei from Mountain Valley, California, noted that these wreaths "added dignity to the memorials held for the deceased and their families."[25]

But artificial flowers sometimes accentuated feelings of marginalization, as in the case of a teenage daughter who watched the health of her diabetic mother worsen at Poston. Having successfully controlled her blood sugar before imprisonment, this fifty-two-year-old wife and mother of five found the camp diet of rice, potatoes, and macaroni disastrous, and eventually it led to her death. Women internees

47. Funeral wreaths at Heart Mountain. Courtesy of the Ethel Ryan
Collection, John Taggert Hinckley Library, Northwest College, Powell,
Wyoming.

attempted to comfort surviving family members by making funeral
flowers from Kleenex, but Akiyo Deloyd looked back on her mother's
funeral with enduring regret because she was unable to place a fresh
flower on her grave.[26] Another Nisei woman, however, found solace in
the paper flowers made by Issei women. After having been released from
camp on a program sponsored by the National Japanese American Student Relocation Council, a daughter returned to Topaz from a college
in Colorado for the funeral of her father, thankful that his coffin was
covered with "cascades" of crepe-paper flowers "painstakingly" made
by Issei women."[27]

Paper flower makers were at the center of a collective response to the
murder of James Hatsuki Wakasa. Shot in the twilight hours of April 11,
1943, by a guard as he approached the barbed-wire fence surrounding
Topaz, sixty-three-year-old Wakasa died immediately. A soldier stationed at sentry tower 8 in the southwest corner of the camp had fired
at Wakasa, who was nearing the western portion of the fence. Accounts

48. Women making artificial flowers, which often provided comfort for those who had experienced a death in their family. Amache, March 6, 1943. Photographer: Pat Coffey. Courtesy of the National Archives and Records Administration.

of the shooting vary, but an autopsy confirmed that Wakasa was shot in the chest while facing the guard rather than while trying to escape. Although insisting that the shooting was justified because Wakasa was attempting to crawl under the fence, administrators and military leaders revealed a convoluted and misapplied sense of culpability when military police stationed at Topaz were placed on "general alert" and armed with machine guns, tear gas, and gas masks. Such an order was an overreaction of enormous proportions when we recall that Japanese Americans imprisoned at Topaz were isolated in the middle of a desert, with little support or resources. As was clear to Japanese Americans incarcerated at Topaz, including Wakasa, an escape attempt in this environment was suicidal. Although Gerald B. Philpott, the guard who shot Wakasa, was reassigned and avoided punishment for his actions, internees imprisoned at Topaz protested by holding a public funeral for the Issei bachelor on April 20, near the location where he was murdered. Women of every block contributed time to creating "enormous" funeral wreaths made with paper flowers. In the context of Wakasa's murder, these works of art were provocative and compelling visual discourses of protest and loss.[28]

Although these art objects expressed the human losses endured by internees, other camp-made art replaced items that had been lost. As Japanese Americans packed up their homes and prepared for the implementation of Executive Order 9066, they made difficult decisions about what to eliminate from overstuffed duffle bags, trunks, and luggage. With Japanese Americans limited to bringing only what they could carry, toys were among the first items left behind in church basements, padlocked barns, and trash piles. Concerned for the well-being and survival of over 60,000 imprisoned youngsters, many internees remained focused, throughout the long years of imprisonment, on creating art objects that engaged the imaginations of youngsters while adsorbing their energy. Enthusiasm for model planes was high among boys of all ages, with youngsters, teenagers, and grown men often joining together to attend classes, compete in meets, and enjoy exhibits. As part of the Anita Funita Festival, an all-camp Fourth of July celebration, Henry Ohye organized a model plane meet that included enthusiasts of all ages and skill levels. Those who participated were separated into four divisions: the hand-launched glide category was best suited for beginners; more experienced crafters found that the flight endurance and speed classes challenged their skill levels; and a "free-for-all" division ensured that any and all internees interested in participating were included. With a large group of crafters and plenty of entries, winning models were disqualified from further competition.[29]

Model plane crafters also gathered informally to enjoy the first flights of newly constructed models, as was the case of a group of twenty-five little boys chasing the latest creation of Tets Kawakami. Made from Kleenex tissue, glue, and balsa wood, the small red plane had taken Kawakami four days to create. Flying over the infield of Santa Anita's racetrack, model planes like Kawakami's were magnets for boys who, anxious to arrive at landing areas, raced along underneath these airborne toys. Always eager to examine the planes up close, youngsters arrived out of breath but insisted on peppering the builder with questions.[30] Model plane enthusiasts at Topaz braved the cold, holding an impromptu "model airplane flying and glider exhibit" on December 27, 1942. Spectators were encouraged to spend an enjoyable Sunday afternoon outside in the frigid air watching camp artists Kenneth Ozawa and Henry Fujita Jr. fly their gliders of balsa wood. Gathered on the grounds of the Topaz high school after lunch, a large crowd of children also witnessed M. Yamashita expertly guide his gas-propelled, motorized model through the sky.[31]

A Tanforan internee ensured a steady stream of supplies by making airplane models for a program sponsored by the U.S. government that trained civilians to identify enemy aircraft. Other interested internees were encouraged to participate with the organizer of the effort, and they reported to the camp newspaper: "If we make the models good enough, we'll be provided with an unlimited supply of materials."[32] Model plane builders at Puyallup likely devised a similar strategy. Launching an all-camp plane-building contest sponsored jointly by the Seattle Civilian War Commission and Frederick and Nelson's department store, Rube Hosokawa announced the arrival of paint, glue, design plans, sandpaper, and pine. Open to internees of all ages and lasting a single week, the competition required participants to choose from a list of Japanese, German, and

49. Boys carving model planes at Poston, October 1943. Photographer unknown. Courtesy of the National Archives and Records Administration.

American warplanes. Completed models were used by civilian air wardens of western Washington in distinguishing between enemy and friendly aircraft. Although models submitted for judging remained the property of the War Commission, the winning entrant received a twenty-five-dollar war savings bond. But the biggest prize was securing more than ample plane-building supplies for Puyallup's crafters.[33] At Manzanar, obtaining model plane supplies from government sources was more difficult. Announcing the formation of classes for making "civilian spotter" models, the *Manzanar Free Press* reported that daily sessions were open to youngsters over the age of twelve. Unfortunately attendance was low because participants were required to provide their own materials and tools for the first batch of planes.[34]

Despite a slow start, Manzanar evolved into one of the most active airplane-model-building camps, with the imaginations of young and old alike perhaps fueled by an active airport directly across Highway

395 from the camp. Built as a U.S. Army facility in 1941, the airport was used to train bomber pilots and test experimental aircraft. When civilian planes traversing western portions of the United States experienced in-flight emergencies, they were rerouted to this isolated airfield with long runways located near Death Valley, California. Most model plane building and flying activities were organized by Manzanar's Wing Nuts club, which held frequent exhibits, classes, and flying demonstrations. Youngsters interested in the art form met every evening from six until dark at block 16, barrack 15, under the supervision of Richard Kunazawa, an expert plane builder.[35] Kunazawa advised his young charges to pay careful attention to the maneuverability, velocity, and appearance of their creations, the three basic precepts of this art form. The gas-propelled and glider models entered into competitions were judged on these elements.[36] Planes of another sort were the concern of Kamso Yamashiro, who built a giant stationary airplane for Santa Anita children. With materials scavenged from mess halls and communal laundry facilities, and using a camp-made hammer, saw, and pocket knife, he fashioned the fuselage out of three apple crates and plated the cowling with flattened tin cans. The wheels were made from round pieces of wood placed inside large tin cans.[37]

Model boats created by incarcerated Japanese Americans were replacements for lost toys, which aided children as they created mental landscapes of survival. In addition to more conventional boat models, a sailboat capable of carrying a skipper and two passengers was built at Lake Tanforan. With an eight-foot-long hull, two outrigger pontoons, a mast eleven feet high, and a sail with a spread of twenty-eight feet, the vessel was the creation of Hisaichi Tsugawa, who before internment had been a fishing boat captain. Made by hallowing out an abandoned telephone pole found on the outskirts of camp, the boat was both buoyant and leak proof, thanks to the materials Tsugawa bought for twelve dollars. After applying five coats of paint and repairing rotten portions of the pole with six pounds of putty, the captain began offering rides to eager children. By July 15, 1942, the vessel was making it's seventy-fifth journey, having capsized three times. In water one-foot deep, the captain reacted to these "spills" by easily hoisting youthful passengers on his shoulders and pulling the boat safely to shore.[38]

Along with model boats and planes, camp-made dolls and kites were perhaps the most common art objects replacing lost toys, and they articulated the internees' need to restore some semblance of childhood to imprisoned youngsters. Most dolls were hand sewn and made with paper, scraps of cloth, and straw, with buttons serving for eyes. A thirteen-year-old girl incarcerated at Rohwer reported in an autobiographical essay for her English class that she spent many happy hours designing clothes for her creations.[39] Making and flying kites were memorialized in an Estelle Ishigo painting titled *Boys with Kite,* which portrayed two little boys untangling their newest creation from a barbed-wire fence. Although Sundays at Lake Tanforan were reserved for model boat enthusiasts, kite crafters took over the area on Saturday afternoons. Prizes were often awarded for the highest flyer as well as the largest, smallest, and most artistic kites. Winners were required to keep their kites airborne for a minimum of ten minutes.[40]

An especially engaging toy for Minidoka's children were painted stones arranged into scenes that communicated fairytales. Ranging in sizes measuring as small as a fingernail to two inches high, these stone toys were played with by children as they learned important life lessons provided by Japanese culture.[41] Although other forms of camp-made toys were less conventional, they were equally popular among imprisoned youngsters. A young women concerned about the lack of toys available to Santa Anita's children raised eyebrows when she rummaged through mess hall trash cans. Concerns were allayed when a reporter for the camp newspaper informed readers that the scavenger, an internee supervisor for the YWCA girls club at Santa Anita, was gathering milk bottle tops, empty cans, and discarded cereal boxes for a toy-making project. Midori Kasai also organized an art class in which imprisoned girls used

50. Girls proudly display the dolls they made at the Labor Day Festival, Newell, California, September 7, 1943. Photographer: Francis Stewart. Courtesy of the National Archives and Records Administration.

these scavenged materials, along with scraps of yarn, cloth, and wire, to make artwork that decorated the interior walls of living quarters.[42]

Nisei teenagers who worked on Santa Anita's camouflage-net project also scavenged materials for toys. Under the direction of the Army Corps of Engineers, over 800 young internees performed dusty and tiring tasks. These workers used their rest periods to collect excess threads from gunny sacks, which they later wound into balls. Through this process, tangled strips of burlap were transformed into tightly wound balls used to play games of catch, dodgeball, soccer, and baseball. Rest periods consumed with making balls can be explained by the demographic of the workers, who were primarily teenagers. According to Kiyoko Ike, camouflage factories were good places to make friends because "hundreds and hundreds of young boys and girls were drafted as workers."[43]

To many readers the task of making balls from these materials may appear mindless, but it was meticulous and intricate work demanding that threads be sorted according to thickness and length. Ball makers also became skilled knot tiers as they connected and tied off end after end. Along with making hundreds of balls for children to play with, Santa Anita's camouflage workers devoted nearly 3,000 work hours to producing over 2,200 nets for the military. The nets varied from between 22 by 24 feet to 36 by 60 feet. With the money saved by producing these nets in such an exploitive work environment, the U.S. government offset the cost of all food consumed at Santa Anita. Even with this contribution by young Nisei internees, working conditions were atrocious, provoking the only strike at any of the temporary imprisonment facilities. A major complaint by these youngsters was a persistent weakness caused by hunger.[44]

Mothers also made and sold crafts as a way to finance what most think of as typical experiences for free youngsters, but in the context of the internment camps these were rare and special events for imprisoned children. At Denson, Arkansas, YWCA Fujin Kai (women's club) members made chenille flowers that were sold by Y members in Little Rock, and the proceeds went toward financing activities for interned youngsters. On rare occasions and only with the approval of camp administrators, these funds paid for trips by young internees to Y activities held beyond the confines of the camp.[45] On August 4, 1943, a member of the Denson Fujin Kai reported to the national office that two members of the Girls' Reserve were permitted to attend a conference in Little Rock and that the group was looking forward to sending another three girls to Gulf Port Summer Camp.[46] At Rohwer women made and sold carnations for Mother's Day gifts, and they used the eighty dollars in profit to send nine girls to the same summer camp.[47]

The loss of pets was an emotionally wrenching experience for children and adults alike. Aiko Tanamachi Endo, who was fifteen years old at the time of internment, later recalled that her saddest memory was disposing of the family dog, a "mutt" with the appearance of a German Shepard.

Because their dog never took kindly to strangers, the Endos realized that their only option was contacting the Humane Society. With all the packing and turmoil in the household, the dog sensed something was wrong and retreated under the house, refusing to come out even to eat. Once the Humane Society arrived, Endo's brother crawled to the frightened animal's hiding place and forcibly dragged the dog to a waiting truck, a depressing scene that left the entire family with disturbing and lasting memories of their loyal and cherished pet.[48]

Another family imprisoned at Tanforan and Topaz was fortunate to find a home for their pedigreed Scotch collie. With most of their friends also destined for the camps, Yoshiko Uchida placed an ad in the University of California, Berkeley, student newspaper, reading: "I am one of the Japanese American students soon to be evacuated and have a male Scotch collie that can't come with me. Can anyone give him a home?" A boy who seemed especially caring was chosen as the new owner of Laddie, but not without much consternation. Especially upsetting for the oldest daughter who was the animal lover of the family, the Uchida's packed up Laddie's doghouse, leash, food bowl, and brushes and sadly said goodbye. Many weeks later the family learned that their loved pet never adapted to his new home and died shortly after the Uchidas were transported to Tanforan.[49]

Sixty years after seeing his dog for the last time, Yoshito Wayne Osaki recalled this painful memory in detail. The dog had been a present from his father, and Osaki named his new "best friend" Teny. A few days before this eighteen-year-old from Courtland, California, was shipped to Tule Lake, Teny vanished, only to reappear when a pickup truck containing the Osaki family pulled into the street to begin the journey that would end with incarceration. Sitting in the back of the pickup on a pile of luggage, Osaki wept as Teny attempted to chase down the truck but failed. Osaki's lasting memory was watching his "constant companion" fall farther and farther behind and finally, after a mile of all-out effort, sitting down in the middle of the road panting heavily.[50] A ten-year-old imprisoned at Rohwer was forced to leave behind her turtle, dogs, cats, canaries, and goldfish. She wrote in her diary: "The pet I liked best was our dog. We gave her to a man but she cut the rope and came home. When we finally left, she cried like anything. We did too."[51]

A teenage girl imprisoned first at Stockton and later Jerome was forced to give her dog to a white neighbor. The knowledge that her pet was going to a good home did not console the young owner, who fought back tears for a second day in a row after saying goodbye to her "best friend."[52] Estelle Ishigo, in her book of drawings and text documenting the lives of internees incarcerated at Pomona and Heart Mountain, memorialized the difficult decisions forced on the pet-owning Japanese Americans. At the very beginning of Lone Heart Mountain, Ishigo describes the experience of six-year-old Kenji, who took his dog on one last walk before the boy was shipped to an "assembly center." Disturbingly, the destination of the walk was a veterinarian's office because no one was willing to take in the aging dog and, according to Ishigo, "because his master is Japanese." Accompanying the text is a drawing of a small boy kneeling by a small mound of dirt grasping a ball once used to play fetch.[53]

Camp crafters addressed these traumas and painful losses by creating works of art. A wooden yard sculpture of a dog created by Karon Sanda was known as the "pet of the neighborhood" and became a favorite of children, who, passing by on their way to and from mess halls, left scraps of bread behind for their new canine friend.[54] A father and his son imprisoned at Tanforan and later at Topaz spent many of their days carving small animal figures from wood and distributing them to children. For internees, especially children, who lost cherished pets, these art forms allowed very personal moments of grief and mental pain to be placed in the open, permitting broader collectivities to bear some of the weight. Children who carried wooden representations of lost pets in their pockets where encouraged to remember and reveal their losses. Here, grief, sorrow, and anguish were materially memorialized for all to see and handle, rather than being pondered and thought out in mental seclusion.

51. Father and son carve small wooden animals, San Bruno, California, June 1, 1942. Photographer: Dorothea Lange. Courtesy of the National Archives and Records Administration.

In this way, enormous pain was partially subdued, even if momentarily, providing spaces in which internees found the strength to open their minds and imagine new mental landscapes and possibilities. Overwhelming sadness and depression caused by experiences such as losing pets was thought over by creating and consuming art. Camp-made art that revealed the loss of pets aided internees in imagining the possibility of surviving their imprisonment experiences with some level of emotional and mental health intact. These works of art helped some internees to create mental spaces of survival that generated new ideas and cultural practices, allowing individual mental anguish to be considered collectively. These works of art addressed the loss of pets and they likely evoked wistful feelings among internees accustomed to warm furry bodies and wet kisses from cherished pets.

Vocational and business losses were pervasive internment experiences, and many internees responded by establishing thriving enterprises in the camps. A Manzanar geta maker who had been a landscape gardener before imprisonment reported that he found purpose in his crafting activities. (Getas, as mentioned earlier, are traditional Japanese footwear, similar to raised wooden sandals, that allow feet to stay dry and mud free.) Japanese American concentration camps were barren and wind-torn landscapes. Most internees recognized getas as "indispensable" because dusty walkways and paths quickly turned to mud during rainy seasons.[55] During their imprisonment many internees began wearing getas for the first time, most commonly as shower clogs, because they allowed the muddy paths between communal bathing facilities, latrines, and living units to be more easily traversed.[56] Even after rock, pebble, and wooden walkways were completed, getas remained popular, with internees using them to combat ever-present foot funguses by wearing the elevated footwear while bathing in communal showers.[57] During the long hot dusty summer days, rain showers were rare and welcome occasions, with internees happily replacing their everyday shoes with getas in order to better navigate muddy areas and carry on their daily activities.[58] Although geta making became a widely practiced art form in the camps, the carving of this footwear was beyond the skills of many imprisoned Japanese Americans. After several "amateurs" at Puyallup, Washington, produced getas that caused shower goers to "endanger life and limb," Toyonosuke Fujikado converted a portion of his already cramped living quarters into a workshop, and during the first few months of imprisonment he provided seven hundred pairs free of charge.[59]

52. Manzanar craftsman making getas, April 2, 1942. Photographer: Clem Albers. Courtesy of the National Archives and Records Administration.

Having lost a thriving sewing business in Stockton, California, Kaoru Ito rejected the offer of working for the War Relocation Authority. Instead she taught ikebana and needlework classes, charging twenty-five cents for each session.[60] In 1919, at the age of fourteen, Ito immigrated to the United States with her parents and soon began working as a "school-girl," a term used for young domestic workers, in the home of Alameda's mayor. On a salary of fifty dollars a month, Ito saved enough money in a single year to attend the Goto Sewing School in Oakland and later the McDowell Sewing School in San Francisco.[61] Concentrating on the arts of design and drafting at McDowell, Ito gained enough experience by 1924 to open her own sewing school in Oakland. As proprietor of the Aileen Sewing School, Ito served a clientele composed primarily of immigrant women who spoke little English.[62] At the age of twenty-five and still single, Ito was encouraged by her parents to marry, and they arranged a meeting for her with her future husband, who resided in Stockton. Although at first hesitant "to move to a town in the hinterlands," Ito finally relented, but not before she notified her future in-laws that she had no intention of working at the family's grocery store and gaining permission to move her sewing business to Stockton. Along with giving birth to three daughters and successfully reestablishing her business in Stockton, Ito was credentialed in 1933 as a teacher of ikebana by the Seizan Goryu school. In 1937, Ito returned to Japan to visit her birthplace, Ota Village in Gunma prefecture, located about one hundred kilometers northwest of Tokyo, but the real purpose of her trip was to receive further training in the art of ikebana.

While interned at Stockton and Rohwer, Ito taught crocheting, knitting, sewing, and ikebana classes, relying on Sears Roebuck and Montgomery Ward mail order catalogs for her needlework supplies and on a wide range of vegetation found in the Arkansas woods for her flower-arranging materials. Located just over one hundred miles southeast of Little Rock and five miles east of the Mississippi River in swampy woodlands, Rohwer was known for its diverse plant life, including many species of wildflowers, shrubs, berries, ferns, vines, and trees, which ikebana enthusiasts eagerly exploited.[63] Ito's crocheting and knitting classes were also popular with women, who were now pressed to quickly make their own sweaters and suits. After being released from Rohwer, Ito returned to Stockton with her family and began working as a domestic, while her husband found employment as a gardener. Ito continued teaching ikebana at the Stockton Buddhist temple, where she and her husband also served as baishakumin or matchmakers. As Ito's experience illustrates, some internees found a way to continue their vocational interests while imprisoned. Although the focus of these art-centered enterprises was not profitability, they helped replace other practical losses endured by internees, such as clothes, curtains, and linens.

Because they were forced by armed soldiers to adhere to a two-bag limit, internees arrived at camp carrying only the necessities of life.[64] Left behind was a whole range of personal possessions, which internees attempted to replace by creating art. Jewelry in the form of shell brooches, bracelets made with flattened pieces of tin cans stenciled with nails, and bird lapel pins made with scrap lumber replaced lost personal items and spoke to internees' needs to add physical and visual diversity to their lives.[65] For persons confined in dry, desolate, and beige environments, the creation of so many colorful and diversely textured artworks likely disturbed the monochrome landscape that enveloped most camps. Portrait drawing evolved into a popular art form, perhaps compensating for the prohibition on cameras enforced by War Relocation Authority officials and armed soldiers. In addition, this practice of creating portraits likely mediated the permanent loss of family photographs left behind when Japanese Americans were forcibly removed from their homes. Crayoned pictures created by imprisoned children replaced cherished artworks carried home from school before internment and saved in scrapbooks and trunks, and hung on the walls of homes. Camp-made carved and polished wooden boxes replaced trinket boxes commonly found in most homes and holding such items as coins, stamps, and writing utensils. In concentration camps these containers were often filled with scavenged nails, playing cards, flower and vegetable seeds, salvaged wire for artificial-flower-making activities, and marbles purchased from mail order catalogs and cherished by many imprisoned children. Containers were also woven from grass gathered on camp grounds and filled with cigarettes, toothpicks, shells for making jewelry, and sewing supplies.

The creation of clothing and fashion accessories such as belts and hats not only addressed the loss of personal possessions but also spoke to practical needs, as in the case of a dress created by an Amache woman, Yukino Tashiro. An enduring memory of Tashiro's daughter was her mother transforming a hundred-pound rice sack into a dress. Struggling with the unruly material, Tashiro was careful to place the red rose decorating the sack on the front of the dress. As her daughter recalled, Tashiro "drew straight lines, cut straight edges, stitched straight seams, just like Yott-chan [her instructor] taught her." Tashiro typically ordered sewing supplies from the *Denver Post*'s Household Arts Department, but for this dress she relied on heavy-duty white mercerized thread brought with her from home. After a long and tiring day taming uncooperative materials, Tashiro hurriedly threw on her newly made garment and rushed to her job bussing tables at one of the mess halls. Responsible for collecting silverware from tables, this mess hall worker found that the addition of a large front pocket proved well worth her time and trouble. Tashiro received a certificate for completing sixty hours of sewing classes, an accomplishment that served her well.[66] Camp-made art often replaced objects left behind as Japanese Americans were forced to dramatically pare down their possessions. Robbed of aesthetics, memories, and functionality encompassed by these objects, internees made camp art to partially recuperate these "things" and the meanings attached to them.

My hope is that this chapter provokes readers to think about art as critical to the mental and psychic health of people living in oppressive conditions. Internees endured losses that ranged from sending family members off to World War II battlefields and the forced abandonment of beloved pets to being deprived of vocational focus and personal belongings. To cope with these losses, some internees linked making and consuming camp-made material cultures with psychic energy. In the context of these immense losses and the attacks on mental well-being that defined everyday life in Japanese American concentration camps, art served as mental spaces of survival by helping internees articulate their most hopeless thoughts and desperate feelings. Art was one method by which internees placed their personal mental struggles in collective arenas, where the loss and psychic agony of individuals were engaged with as a group.

Rather than remaining within the solitary confines of individual minds, personal torments evolved into social behavior, collective

53. Bird lapel pins made from scrap wood. Courtesy of the Rosalie Santine Gould Collection

considerations, and cultural practices. As the most basic exercise of identity building, this process illuminates how art urged individuals to construct new understandings of themselves and then connect these understanding to larger collectivities. A strategy for holding on in desperate circumstances, camp crafting activities improved the likelihood that internees would avoid complete mental devastation. Art aided in forming mental spaces where all-consuming sadness was quieted, even if fleetingly, allowing some internees to think about how to establish some level of agency in their lives. Difficult to capture in words, internment losses and mental anguish were perhaps best articulated through art that varied dramatically in form, aesthetics, and materials. Here, we again see difference playing out materially, allowing a heterogeneous group of people to choose and construct visions and discourses that best suited their interests and concerns.

CHAPTER 6

Contemporary Legacies
of Loss

As this book concludes, I urge readers to think about art created in Japanese American concentration camps with five ideas. First is the function and purposes of this work for internees, a historical view grounded in the realities of everyday life and imprisonment. Second is the idea of loss, which is critical for moving camp-made art into the present and future instead of understanding these artifacts as belonging solely to the past. Third is the idea of art, broadly defined, as creating portable spaces in which a sense of place can be at least partially recuperated. This framework addresses transnational flows of people as they are forced to ground themselves in often hostile and unfamiliar landscapes. Through this lens, we focus on understanding the historical and cultural contexts that inform global, national, and local movements (or non-movements, as the case may be) of people and resources.

The final two ideas involve more intellectual issues that likely will resonate most deeply with students of material culture but are equally applicable for museum goers. Addressing the meanings and uses of artifactual evidence, this fourth idea urges readers to think about how museums often have conservative influences on artifacts by constructing narrow narratives to be consumed by the public. My fifth and final idea proposes a more active perspective, suggesting that artifacts encompass powers that evoke responses from people. Here, we find artifacts encompassing agency. Instead of constructing a singular narrative, artifacts can

154

generate ideas and be employed to confront present-day conditions of marginalization and exploitation. As I suggest in these concluding pages, each of these ideas is central to the historical meanings and contemporary uses of art created in Japanese American concentration camps.

Camp-made art held critical meanings and served essential functions for both makers and consumers. As internees employed art to remake interior places and outside spaces, maintain and create human connections, and construct new psychic landscapes, they bolstered their prospects of physically and mentally surviving the many traumas encompassed by Executive Order 9066. By studying the lived experiences of internees, we see that art is about more than aesthetics. Camp-made material cultures turned the individual and personal into the social, allowing internees to construct visual conversations about matters perhaps too painful to discuss verbally. Serving as critical spaces of survival and revealing contexts of overwhelming loss, camp-made art encompassed ideas, strategies, and practices ranging from the practical to the political. Drawing on losses rooted in the historical and oppressive histories of Japanese Americans, these artifacts can be connected with injustices occurring in contemporary contexts. In much the same way that internees offered their art to each other for collective consideration, they also provided lasting inheritances for succeeding generations to think with. In this way, those of us interested in advancing progressive social justice causes can reconsider our collective present and future. Although these artful practices were firmly rooted in the past and have specific historical meanings, camp artists also created narratives of loss and melancholic agency for the present.

Recent scholarship based on Sigmund Freud's theory of mourning and melancholia points to the intellectual, cultural, and political meanings of loss. Freud described mourning as a temporary reaction to loss.[1] While mourning is a process in which the mourner eventually moves on, melancholia is a loss that one cannot get over. Melancholia is an enduring condition, a mourning without end, and according to Freud,

pathological.[2] But some cultural scholars such as David Karzanjian and
David Eng suggest that "melancholic attachments to loss" encompass
creative impulses that reveal social contexts and political possibilities. By
depathologizing and reinterpreting Freud's melancholia, we are offered
views of unresolveable and politicized struggles with loss. Exploring the
practices through which loss is melancholically materialized, we can
begin to understand art created by imprisoned Japanese Americans as
encompassing half lives that continue to work in the present and future.
As much as we may want to escape memories and realities of historical loss, avoidance is an impossible task. In the words of Judith Butler,
"the past is not past."[3] This interpretation of melancholia challenges
assumptions that loss and grief reside solely in the psychological realm
and moves these matters to the social and political. Although the losses
of Japanese Americans are irrecoverable, we can employ them to inform
our futures.

Losses experienced by Japanese Americans resonate in the present
because they keep melancholic struggles alive and relevant. With their
melancholic attachments, internees revealed and asserted their many
losses for all to see. Past injustices are remembered and revisited through
works of art created in environments of loss such as the Japanese American concentration camps. As a former fisherman from Terminal Island,
California, recounted, the model boat he made at Manzanar from orange
and apple crates was built as a "reminder of the imprisonment of one
hundred and twenty thousand innocent Japanese Americans."[4] Camp-
made art helps us recognize that we must continually revisit past losses
not with the goal of resolution but by acknowledging that these losses
will never be totally erased, exorcized, or banished. Rather, we must
embrace these engagements with loss because this process helps us as we
attempt to imagine and create more humane futures.

It is through these exercises of returning to historical losses that we
think out new social, cultural, economic, and political possibilities. Just
as some internees employed art to piece together alternative dialogues

and generate new ideas to survive with, contemporary readers can draw on these visual conversations to construct more options for the future. These artifacts, often thought of as belonging to the past, can kindle new thoughts, practices, and tactics to deal with current challenges. As residues of loss, camp-made works of art provoke our memories and raise questions about present-day conditions of oppression. We must continue to look back with melancholic visions, like those provided by camp artists, as we learn to create enduring social change. Loss, in its many forms, must therefore be an ever-present shadow around our hearts and minds as we seek to enact new visions for human liberation.

These accounts of loss are especially critical when we consider current environments that are similar to those experienced by Japanese Americans imprisoned in U.S. concentration camps during World War II. Civil rights infringements targeted at Arab and Muslim Americans have been carried out by the U.S. government most specifically through the authorization of the Patriot Act in 2001 and its reauthorization in 2006. The increase in hate crimes and media bias directed toward these groups has been well documented, as has the use of census data to racially identify Americans of Arab descent. Attacks on Arab and Muslim Americans continue to rise in post-9/11 environments. During 2005 the Council on American-Islamic Relations processed 1,972 complaints of anti-Muslim harassment, violence, and discriminatory treatment, an all time high in reported civil rights abuses. These numbers represent a 30 percent increase from 2004, when 1,522 such events were recorded. Reports of anti-Muslim hate crimes rose to 153, a nearly 10 percent increase over those reported in 2004 and a 65 percent increase over the 93 such crimes reported in 2003. Racial profiling and unreasonable detention were the most common civil rights complaints. Hate crimes included the bombing of a Cincinnati mosque, the beating by teenagers of an elderly man as he left an Arizona mosque, and the assault on a pregnant woman in Virginia by three men who shouted anti-Muslim slurs. According to several public opinion surveys, anti-Muslim sentiment continues to rise, with over half of those polled expressing negative views of Islam and one in four openly conveying "extreme" hate of Muslims.[5]

Government surveillance of Muslim and Arab Americans has been easily accomplished through the Patriot Act, which expanded executive branch power. As a result, the gathering of domestic intelligence is a common, everyday occurrence in the United States. Electronic eaves-dropping and almost unfettered access to phone records have led to a National Security Agency database of domestic phone calls. Using what is believed to be the largest database in the world, intelligence officials can easily track the telecommunications of Americans. The collection of this type of information is a clear violation of the Fourth Amendment's protection against "unreasonable searches and seizures," and before leg-islative enactment of the Patriot Act such activities had required a search warrant.[6] Justifying that the compilation of this data was needed to fight terrorism, the government has yet to explain why millions of Americans, most whom were not suspected of any illegal activity, found themselves targets of such draconian measures.

Comparisons with civil rights abuses inflicted on Japanese Americans are impossible to ignore in light of the 2002 and 2003 decisions of the Census Bureau to give the Department of Homeland Security detailed information on Arab Americans.[7] With the Census Bureau's apology in 2000 for allowing census information to be used as a method of quickly and efficiently tracking down and imprisoning innocent Japanese Americans after the bombing of Pearl Harbor, these recent collabora-tions between U.S. intelligence services and census takers are especially troubling. In response to a Freedom of Information Act inquiry, heavily redacted documents were provided to the Electronic Privacy Information Center, a public interest research group focused on civil liberties issues. One document included a tabulation of over a thousand pages that cor-relates zip codes with people of Arab ancestry. These statistical data were further broken down into ethnic categories, including Egyptian, Iraqi, Jordanian, Lebanese, Moroccan, Palestinian, Syrian, Arab/Arabic, and

Other Arab.[8] Compiled from the 2000 census and specifically for the Department of Homeland Security, these special tabulations suggest that census data could once again assist in serious breaches of human rights based on racial identity.

Recalling visual dialogues of loss such as those created by camp-made art can help us as we challenge the human suffering encompassed by present-day displacements and oppression. Refugee emergencies in Laos, Burma, and Sudan, along with many others, continue to challenge human rights organizations and structures of nation-states. A good example are the experiences of the Hmong, an ethnic minority in Laos, many of whom fought alongside U.S. soldiers against Communist forces during the Vietnam War. With the United States' withdrawal from Saigon in April 1975, these Hmong were left in Laos to defend themselves. Hoping to escape genocide, many undertook arduous and life-threatening journeys, fleeing on foot into the high Laotian mountains or across the Mekong River into Thai refugee camps. For those who survived the journey, life in refugee camps was harsh at best, with the Hmong enduring crowded physical environments and food shortages for months and in some cases years.

Although many Hmong now live in diasporic contexts around the world, including communities in the United States, Australia, France, Germany, and Canada, others continue to escape oppressive conditions in Laos by finding their way to refugee camps in Thailand. What the Thai government refers to as an "unofficial refugee settlement" is growing on the roadsides surrounding Huay Nam Khao. Located in northern Thailand's Phetchabin province just across the border with Laos, Huay Nam Khao has drawn what some estimate to be 8,000 Hmong fleeing Laos, many of whom hope to eventually gain U.S. citizenship. Huddled along the roadside and under shelters made from plastic sheathing and corrugated metal panels, these new Hmong refugees endure hunger, crowding, and unsanitary conditions. Recently, 163 were forcibly returned to Laos.[9]

Many Hmong refugees, like the Japanese Americans imprisoned in U.S. concentration camps, have created art that both reflects and shapes their experiences as refugees and speaks to their many losses. For centuries, Hmong women have created embroidery and textiles known as pa ndau. Before the refugee experience, pa ndau were embroidered on clothing to mark rites of passage such as courtship, marriage, birth, and death. During the refugee experience, the art of pa ndau changed from geometric designs embroidered on brightly colored clothes to what are now known as story cloths, which detail narratives of escape and exile from Laos to refugee camps in Thailand. Story cloths entered the economic realm when they were created as commodities for sale to Westerners. These works of art have become the material means of survival for many Hmong living in refugee camps and continue to represent a means of support among Hmong Americans.

Burma's Karen refugees, who were driven from their rural villages by Burmese military forces, are currently surviving in camps along the Thai-Burmese border. Seven camps house 140,000 Karen refugees, while another 150,000 are internally displaced just inside Burma's border. As an ethnic minority, the Karen population is fighting for political autonomy and hoping to establish a state of its own free from repression by the Burmese government. In Darfur, genocidal conditions also highlight challenges we must address as more than two million people are currently displaced from their homes. And of course there are the more than four million Iraqis who are on the move as result of the Iraq War. Half of these refugees currently live in neighboring countries such as Syria and Jordan, while the other two million endure internal displacement, fleeing to safer regions within Iraq.[10] Finally, in the United States we have examples of severe losses that accompanied the displacement of more than one million Katrina survivors who were separated from family members and scattered across the South.

As the world confronts the many losses created by these and many other forced displacements, historical narratives such as those produced in Japanese American concentration camps provide vital ideas, strategies, and tools. Those of us concerned with addressing global oppressions will be well served to revisit the artful dialogues created by imprisoned Japanese Americans. Along with contemporary accounts of Karen, Hmong, Darfur, and Iraqi refugees, artwork created in Japanese American concentration camps helps us to reveal political possibilities and create more liberative futures for people who find themselves in environments of loss. All of these experiences reckon back to the imprisonment of Japanese Americans, who struggled to reveal and mediate the many losses caused by Executive Order 9066. As in the case of imprisoned Japanese Americans, residues of the immense losses created by contemporary oppressions and displacements will be melancholically revealed for years to come.

Placing art in transnational contexts, the third idea this book offers readers, helps us understand how displaced groups of people establish portable senses of place. By pushing our understanding of place beyond fixed and confined space, we set place in motion. Thinking with the idea of movement loosens place making from physical boundaries, to incorporate and reflect the diverse experiences of displaced refugee and immigrant populations. In the case of some imprisoned Japanese Americans, a sense of place was carried with them and then enacted in the spaces of camp-made material cultures. Creating art aided internees in a process of re-territorialization by altering living units, collective gathering spaces, and outside landscapes into more survivable places. Although life remained difficult and painful, creating art helped internee crafters take advantage of rare opportunities where exerting even limited amounts of control was possible. Many camp artists utilized the resources offered by particular landscapes and relied on found materials. At Topaz and Tule Lake, women sifted through prehistoric lake beds to gather tiny shells from which brooches and decorative plaques were made. Kobu evolved into a meaningful art form at Rohwer and Jerome, Arkansas. Discarded fruit crates were critical to furniture makers, weeds and grasses were used by weavers to make hats, and mud provided material for sculptures and dishes. In this way, imprisoned Japanese Americans employed physical landscapes to remake place.

As marginalized groups of people become increasingly mobile in response to the labor demands of global capitalism, we are urged to think about how place is carried with them and to consider the political and ideological meanings of place and space. Material culture created by such groups may help us better understand the meanings of place to people on the move. Gaining this knowledge is critical because it can help create liberative spaces for displaced people confronting harsh and exploitive environments. Essential to this goal is understanding place as fluid and operating in conditions that are contingent on diverse historical, economic, cultural, and political contexts. Here, conventional thoughts about place as bounded and static are disturbed to create knowledge about how people experiencing dislocations recuperate a sense of place and express some level of agency in their lives, even when this power is severely restricted.

The final two ideas I laid out earlier in the chapter are closely related and address the power infused in artifacts and how physical objects are employed by curators who create exhibits. In museum settings, artifacts are often accompanied by contextualizing text that teaches a specific and unified history to the masses. As especially powerful discourses of nation building, these interpretations are fixed and usually communicate a linear narrative grounded in melting pot ideology. Here we must ask whose story is being told and who is doing the telling. Rather than using artifacts to think with and generate ideas that can be applied to contemporary challenges, museum administrators appear more comfortable placing their collections firmly in the domain of professionals and experts. Physical objects that are rich in ambiguities, gray areas, and questions are presented as encompassing more static and frozen meanings.

Kristine Yuki Aono's 1991 installation "Relics from Camp" illustrates how museums can project more fluid and ruptured interpretations of artifacts.[11] Displayed in a large rectangular wooden container sitting flat on the floor, camp-made objects were arranged in a grid of twelve boxes organized into three rows. Resembling the rows of pine and black tar-papered barracks that characterized camp architecture, the grid was made from wood and painted black. In these boxes lay "camp relics" such as a Tule Lake baseball jersey, a nameplate, carved wooden panels, lapel pins, and dolls made by imprisoned Japanese Americans. That these artifacts were resting in sand implies their grounding in a material that defined camp landscapes and suggests the "undeniable physical reality" of internment. Contextualizing narratives for each object are absent, allowing multiple meanings to be more easily created. With this exhibit of artifacts, museum goers are offered more open interpretations of culture and history. Artifacts displayed in this manner urge museum goers to be more active makers of meaning and more energetic consumers of history. This encouragement to vigorously engage and think with artifactual evidence creates a dialogue between museum curator and museum goer. Exhibits such as Aono's provide an atmosphere where we can value difference and variation in human experience rather than relying so heavily on sameness to interpret the past and present.

Leaving room for the creation of multiple narratives leads us to developing theories and frameworks that assign some level of agency or power to artifacts. Agency is a concept firmly associated with humans. Although most contemporary scholars remain comfortable with the notion that material culture reflects or mirrors history, many are hesitant to argue that artifacts exert agency in shaping culture and human behavior. But this position raises important questions: If the physical world and artifacts do not have the power to create change, why are we studying them? Are we only interested in artifacts for their value as mirrors of history? And more important, is creating knowledge for knowledge's sake a justifiable position for scholars of material culture? Perhaps thinking from new frameworks of agency will help us create politically charged scholarship aimed at revealing new options and strategies that challenge present-day injustices. This is not to argue that artifactual agency is the same as human agency. Rather it is a call to create new theories of agency that relate to material culture and physical objects.

E. McClung Fleming pointed to these possibilities in his 1974 essay titled "Artifact Study: A Proposed Model." While outlining an exhaustive blueprint for interpreting artifacts, Fleming raised the question of agency by writing: "In some cases functional analysis will indicate the ways in which the artifact became an agent of major change within its culture." Here, he introduces the idea that artifacts not only reflect but also shape history and culture.[12] Few have taken up this call to reveal artifactual agency, possibly because of this concept's connection to humans, but it may represent a significant direction for future research. Although practitioners of material culture studies are skilled at identifying moments of artifactual significance, we are less successful at linking these seemingly isolated instances to broader, politically progressive change. We can begin by asking ourselves how we create material culture scholarship that transports liberative change beyond specific locations, historical eras and contemporary moments, and groups of people? Reworking this idea of human agency may help material culture scholars better understand the power infused in artifacts.

Japanese American concentration camp art provides fertile evidence of artifactual agency. Many internees used art to express counternarratives and improve their lives. Without enlisting a diverse range of art forms to create survivable mental and physical landscapes, many imprisoned Japanese Americans would have found their lives even more difficult and trying. By visually and materially enacting what was in their minds, internees revealed social contexts and political possibilities. This argument, of course, challenges understandings of art as frivolous activities that serve only to occupy leisure time. Instead of assuming this trajectory, let us employ art created by Japanese Americans to reveal alternative and liberative practices for creating changes that reach beyond immediate needs, locations, and isolated points of identity. Camp-made

CONTEMPORARY LEGACIES OF LOSS

art, broadly defined, offers powerful examples of how people with little institutionalized power confront complex systems of oppression.

Thinking with art may aid those of us interested in creating enduring social change to find a wide range of voices, strategies, and practices in an often hostile world. My hope is that camp-made material cultures urge contemporary readers to think about the significance of creative expression for marginalized people. Rather than contributing to one grand, linear narrative of Japanese Americans or, on a broader scale, of Asian America, my hope is that *Artifacts of Loss* encourages readers to reveal radical possibilities infused in Japanese American concentration camp art. But this book represents only one interpretation to think with. I encourage you to use this work to develop other readings and to think about art, material culture, and craft making with different eyes and motivations. Beginning to conceive of art as critical to mental and physical survival may help us better understand how people identify fissures in complex systems of oppression, where even limited levels of agency can be expressed. There is much left to study and learn about art and its political trajectories.

Notes

CHAPTER 1 — VISUAL ACCOUNTS OF LOSS

1. Samuel Ichiye Hayakawa was born in Vancouver, British Columbia, on July 18, 1906, of Japanese immigrant parents. Hayakawa immigrated to the United States in 1926 and received a Ph.D. in English and American literature from the University of Wisconsin in 1935. Hayakawa supported the internment of Japanese Americans but avoided imprisonment himself, instead spending the years between 1939 and 1947 at the Armour Institute of Technology (now the Illinois Institute of Technology) in Chicago as an English professor. Best known academically for his work in linguistics, Hayakawa published *Language in Action* in 1941. Between 1955 and 1968 he was a professor of English at San Francisco State College, and in 1968 Governor Ronald Reagan appointed him president of the college. Hayakawa quickly garnered national attention by severely restricting student protests on campus. After retiring from this position in 1973, Hayakawa successfully ran as a Republican candidate for the U.S. Senate in 1976. As a single-term senator from California, Hayakawa introduced a constitutional amendment designating English as the official language of the United States. In 1983, he founded U.S. English, Inc., an organization presently comprised of 1.8 million members. See the organization's Web site, http://www.us-english.org (accessed March 21, 2008). *Biographical Directory of the American Congress, 1774–1996*, s.v. "Samuel Ichiye Hayakawa," http://library.cqpress.com (accessed March 21, 2008).

2. The power of language is a central issue in internment research, with scholars and the public debating use of the words *internment, relocation, evacuation,* and *concentration camp*. I use *internment* and *concentration* camps interchangeably, but by this choice I do not intend a comparison with Nazi concentration

167

camps, which I would argue are more accurately described as death camps. Japanese American internment camps were spatial expressions of race based on concentrating people of Japanese ancestry in geographically specific sites. With this definition in mind, it seems to me that *concentration camp* best describes the outcome of Executive Order 9066 signed by President Franklin D. Roosevelt on February 19, 1942.

3. Sam Hayakawa, testimony before the Commission on Wartime Relocation and Internment of Civilians, Los Angeles, August 4, 1981, reel 2, 5–22, National Archives and Records Administration, College Park, MD.

4. My understanding of reterritorialization is grounded in the work of Akhil Gupta and James Ferguson, who urge scholars to consider the conditions of globalization and postmodernity as they relate to the relationships among geography, culture, and identity formation. Akhil Gupta and James Ferguson, "Beyond 'Culture': Space, Identity, and the Politics of Difference," *Cultural Anthropology* 7 (1992): 6–9. Rick Bonus took up Gupta and Ferguson's challenge by studying the experiences of first-generation Filipino Americans in San Diego and Los Angeles. In his work, Bonus suggests that identities be conceptualized as fluid and contingent upon movements between physical locations. In this context, a singular, unifying Filipino American identity is reconceptualized as multiple Filipino American identities formed in specific times and spaces. Re-territorialization thus becomes the process by which hostile spaces are altered into arenas of identity articulation where marginalized people declare differences and enact subjectivity. Rick Bonus, *Locating Filipino Americans: Ethnicity and the Cultural Politics of Space* (Philadelphia: Temple University Press, 2000), 4–5, 77.

5. Gupta and Ferguson, "Beyond 'Culture,'" 17.

6. Miranda Joseph, *Against the Romance of Community* (Minneapolis: University of Minnesota Press, 2002), xxiii.

7. I base my thinking here on Sigmund Freud's theory of mourning and melancholia and recent scholarship pointing to the intellectual, cultural, and political meanings of loss. Freud described mourning as a temporary reaction to loss. Whereas mourning is a process in which the mourner eventually moves on, melancholia is a loss that one cannot get over. Melancholia is an enduring condition, a mourning without end, and according to Freud, pathological. But some cultural scholars such as David Kazanjian and David Eng suggest that melancholic attachments to loss encompass creative impulses that reveal social contexts and political possibilities. By reinterpreting Freud's melancholia, we are offered new views of unresolvable and politicized struggles with loss. David L. Eng and David Kazanjian, eds., *Loss: The Politics of Mourning* (Berkeley: University of California Press, 2003).

8. *Cambridge Dictionary*, http://dictionary.cambridge.org (accessed March 21, 2008). *Webster's New Collegiate Dictionary* defines art as the "conscious use of skill and creative imagination especially in the production of aesthetic objects." *Webster's Eleventh New Collegiate Dictionary* (Springfield, MA: G. and C. Merriam, 2005), 63. The word *art* derives from the Latin word meaning "to arrange." The 1994–2002 *Encyclopedia Britannica* offers that art is "the use of skill and imagination in the creation of aesthetic objects, environments, or experiences that can be shared with others."

9. Deborah Gesensway and Mindy Roseman, *Beyond Words: Images from America's Concentration Camps* (Ithaca: Cornell University Press, 1987); Kimi Kodani Hill, *Topaz Moon: Chiura Obata's Art of the Internment* (Berkeley: Heyday Books, 2000); Kristine Kim, *Henry Sugimoto: Painting an American Experience* (Berkeley: Heyday Books, 2000); Karin M. Higa, *The View from Within: Japanese American Art from the Internment Camps, 1942–1945* (Seattle: University of Washington Press, 1992). Other examples of scholarship on internment art include Karin M. Higa, *Living in Color: The Art of Hideo Date* (Berkeley: Heyday Books, 2001); Robert J. Maeda, "Isamu Noguchi: 5–7-A, Poston, Arizona," *Amerasia Journal* 20, no. 2 (1994): 61–76; Dominique Leblond, "The Sacralization of the American Deserts in the War Relocation Authority Camps for Japanese Americans," *American Studies in Scandinavia* 31, no. 22 (1993): 1–12; Kristine C. Kuramitsu, "Internment and Identity in Japanese American Art," *American Quarterly* 47 (December 1995): 619–658; Josephine Withers, "No More War: An Art Essay," *Feminist Studies* 7, no. 1 (Spring 1981): 76–88.

10. Allen H. Eaton, *Beauty behind Barbed Wire: The Arts of the Japanese in Our War Relocation Camps* (New York: Harper and Brothers, 1952); Delphine Hirasuna, *The Art of Gaman: Arts and Crafts from the Japanese American Internment Camps, 1942–1946* (Berkeley: Ten Speed Press, 2005).

11. Eaton, *Beauty behind Barbed Wire*, 16; Elaine Kim, "Interstitial Subjects: Asian American Visual Art as a Site for New Cultural Conversations," in *Fresh Talk/Daring Gazes: Conversation on Asian American Art*, ed. Elaine H. Kim, Margo Machida, and Sharon Mizota (Berkeley: University of California Press, 2003), 9; Hill, *Topaz Moon*, 46; Valerie Matsumoto, "Japanese American Women during World War II," in *Unequal Sisters: A Multi-Cultural Reader in U.S. Women's History*, ed. Vicki L. Ruiz and Ellen Carol DuBois (New York: Routledge, 1994), 441; Higa, *View from Within*, 22; Edward H. Spicer, Asael T. Hansen, Katherine Luomala, and Marvin Opler, *Impounded People: Japanese-Americans in the Relocation Center* (Tucson: University of Arizona Press, 1969), 217–18; Audrie Girdner and Anne Loftis, *The Great Betrayal: The Evacuation of the Japanese-Americans during World War II* (New York: Macmillan, 1969), 308;

Kuramitsu, "Internment and Identity in Japanese American Art," 637; Charles Kikuchi, *The Kikuchi Diary: Chronicle from an American Concentration Camp* (Urbana: University of Illinois Press, 1993), 135, 204.

12. Fred Barbashi, "Manzanar: Internees' Lives Amid Barbed Wire and Barracks," *Washington Post,* December 6, 1982, A4.

13. Eaton, *Beauty behind Barbed Wire,* 4, 18.

14. Kim, "Interstitial Subjects," 2.

15. Helaine Fendelman and Jonathan Taylor, *Tramp Art: A Folk Art Phenomenon* (New York: Stewart, Tabori and Chang, 1999).

16. Paul Arnett and William Arnett, eds., *Souls Grown Deep: African American Vernacular Art of the South* (Atlanta: Tinwood Books, 2000), 1:270.

17. Rhode Island School of Design, Museum of Art, *Mountain Artisans: An Exhibition of Patchwork and Quilting, Appalachia* (Providence: Rhode Island School of Design, 1970).

18. Jacqueline L. Tobin and Raymond G. Dobard, *Hidden in Plain View: A Secret Story of Quilts and the Underground Railroad* (New York: Anchor Books, 2000), 67.

19. Brian Niiya, ed., *Encyclopedia of Japanese American History: An A–Z Reference from 1868 to the Present* (New York: Checkmark Books, 2001), 126; Jeffery Burton, Mary Farrell, Florence Lord, and Richard Lord, *Confinement and Ethnicity: An Overview of World War II Japanese American Relocation Sites* (Seattle: University of Washington Press, 2002), 376, 352.

20. Haru Isaki, public testimony before the Commission on Wartime Relocation and Internment of Civilians, Seattle, September 9, 1981, reel 4, 267, National Archives and Records Administration.

21. "One must walk a full block to the laundry, then carry the wet wash back a block to hang out on lines. Really, it is quite an ordeal" (Kikuchi, *Kikuchi Diary,* 204). "Dusty roads. Dusty room. Everything is dust-covered: clothing, bedding, our body. Everything soils so easy, it seems washing must be done daily"; Hatsuye Egami, *The Evacuation Diary of Hatsuye Egami,* ed. Claire Gorfinkel (Pasadena, CA: Intentional Productions, 1996), 39, 40. "For mothers with babies and the very old or sick, living was especially hard. With day and night trips to the laundry for water, the mess halls and the latrine barracks"; Estelle Ishigo, *Lone Heart Mountain* (Los Angeles: Baker and Taylor, 1972), 25.

22. Yoshiko Uchida, *Desert Exile: The Uprooting of a Japanese-American Family* (1982; repr., Seattle: University of Washington Press, 2000), 69–70, 114.

23. Letter to Rose Terlin, May 11, 1942, YWCA Records, no. 025–18, box 48, folder 2, 2, Sophia Smith Collection, Smith College.

24. Jack Matsuoka, *Poston: Camp II, Block 211* (San Mateo, CA: Asian American Curriculum Project, 2003), 67–68.

25. Lillie Y. McCabe, interview by Jeffrey B. Yamada, October 19, 1987, Nisei Experience, O.H. 1949, 2, Oral History Program, Japanese American Project, California State University, Fullerton.

CHAPTER 2 — REMAKING INSIDE PLACES

1. "Comfort was uppermost in the minds of the people"; Mine Okubo, *Citizen 13660* (Seattle: University of Washington Press, 1983), 137. William Kimura, public testimony before the Commission on Wartime Relocation and Internment of Civilians, Anchorage, September 15, 1981, reel 6, 84, National Archives and Records Administration, College Park, MD. Martha Inouye Oye, in *Reflections: Memoirs of Japanese American Women in Minnesota*, ed. John Nobuya Tsuchida (Covina, CA: Pacific Asia Press, 1994), 294. As Martha Inouye Oye remembered of her experiences at Minidoka: "Comfort was uppermost in the minds of the people when they first arrived here. As at the assembly centers, talented and creative evacuees built partitions and furniture from discarded lumber and material picked up around the barracks to make their rooms more habitable."

2. Akiyo Deloyd, public testimony before the Commission on Wartime Relocation and Internment of Civilians, Los Angeles, August 4, 1981, reel 2, 87, National Archives and Records Administration.

3. Monica Sone, *Nisei Daughter* (Seattle: University of Washington Press, 2000), 173–174.

4. Mas Ueysugi, interview by John McFarlane, April 16, 1971, Japanese American Evacuation, O.H. 1071, 5, Oral History Program, Japanese American Project, California State University, Fullerton (OHP-CSUF).

5. Violet De Cristoforo, in *And Justice for All: An Oral History of the Japanese American Detention Camps*, ed. John Tateishi, 124–140 (Seattle: University of Washington Press, 1999), 126.

6. Tsuyako Kitashima, public testimony before the Commission on Wartime Relocation and Internment of Civilians, San Francisco, August 13, 1981, reel 3, 168, National Archives and Records Administration; Okubo, *Citizen 13660*, 106.

7. Roy Nagata to Alice Sinclair Dodge, July 30, 1942, box 1, Correspondence 1942–1946 file, Alice Sinclair Dodge Collection, Hoover Institution, Stanford University.

8. For especially vivid descriptions of the train trip from Tanforan to Topaz, see Okubo, *Citizen 13660*, 116–120; and Yoshiko Uchida, *Desert Exile: The*

Uprooting of a Japanese-American Family (1982; repr., Seattle: University of Washington Press, 2000), 102–105.

9. Uchida, *Desert Exile*, 75, 93. Known for her optimistic view of life at Tulare, Hatsuye Egami described her new home as "a rustic barrack of rough boards put together with five windows and a concrete floor. Eight people occupy our room." Egami's positive outlook is mentioned in the introduction to Hatsuye Egami, *The Evacuation Diary of Hatsuye Egami*, ed. Claire Gorfinkel (Pasadena, CA: Intentional Productions, 1996), 15; quote at 26.

10. Minoru Kiyota, *Beyond Loyalty: The Story of a Kibei*, trans. Linda Klepinger Keenan (Honolulu: University of Hawai'i Press, 1997), 76.

11. Http://www.nps.gov/manz/cctopaz (accessed February 15, 2008).

12. Estelle Ishigo, *Lone Heart Mountain* (Los Angeles: Anderson, Ritchie, and Simon, 1972), 19–22.

13. Fusaye Hashimoto, interview by Mary Tamura, February 1994, Terminal Island History Project, Japanese American National Museum, Los Angeles, 7–8; Tomitaro and Mrs. Marumoto, interview by Toshiro Izumi, March 10, 1994, Terminal Island History Project, Japanese American National Museum, 9.

14. Anonymous, interview by Richard Curtiss, March 4, 1966, Japanese American Evacuation, O.H. 11, 9, OHP-CSUF.

15. Carey McWilliams, "What about Our Japanese-Americans?" *Catholic Digest*, May 1944, 22.

16. Himi Hashimoto, Rohwer autobiography no. 57, English 11-B, December 10, 1942, Gould/Vogel Collection, McGehee, AR.

17. Egami, *Evacuation Diary*, 60.

18. "From Cooking to Carpentry," *Tanforan Totalizer*, June 20, 1942, 5.

19. Sone, *Nisei Daughter*, 175.

20. Ibid., 182. Other references to illegal hotplates are found in Okubo, *Citizen 13660*, 67; Ishigo, *Lone Heart Mountain*, 12.

21. With limited ingredients and no refrigeration, internees relied on catalog orders and supplies sent from friends back home to make dishes such as chocolate ice cream from cans of condensed milk, honey, and chocolate flavoring. Once the chocolate was melted, the ingredients were whipped together and left outside to freeze. A recipe for "rum tum ditty" suggested combining tomato soup, tuna, and Parmesan cheese, while a complete dinner was composed of mushroom soup, toasted cheese sandwiches, pickles, coffee, jello with canned fruit, and cookies for dessert. Successful completion of the cheese sandwiches required "inveigling your dining hall into giving you a loaf of bread." Marii Kyogoku, "A la Mode," *Trek*, December 1942, 27; and Evelyn Kirimura, "Food Fancies," *Topaz Times*, January 16, 1943, 5; February 6, 1943, 5; March 20, 1943, 5.

22. Janet Sato, Rohwer autobiography no. 162, period 2, December 1942, Gould/Vogel Collection.

23. U.S. Army, Western Defense Command and Fourth Army, *Final Report: Japanese Evacuation from the West Coast, 1942* (Washington, DC: Government Printing Office, 1943), 227.

24. Kimura, public testimony, 84.

25. Nobuko Hanzawa, Rohwer autobiography no. 135, English 4, period 2, December 1942; George Kobayashi, Rohwer autobiography no. 67, English 11-B, December 14, 1942; both in the Gould/Vogel Collection.

26. Florence Miho Nakamura, "Barrack in Tanforan," in *From Our Side of the Fence: Growing Up in America's Concentration Camps*, by the Japanese Cultural and Community Center of Northern California, ed. Brian Komei Dempster (San Francisco: Kearny Street Workshop Press, 2001), 42.

27. "Out of the Horse's Mouth," *Tanforan Totalizer,* May 15, 1942, 2.

28. Tule Lake and Manzanar served as both temporary and permanent imprisonment facilities.

29. Charles Kikuchi, *The Kikuchi Diary: Chronicle from an American Concentration Camp,* ed. John Modell (Urbana: University of Illinois Press, 1993), 248, 250.

30. Uchida, *Desert Exile,* 99–100.

31. Yoshio Matsuda, Rohwer autobiography no. 70, December 14, 1942, Gould/Vogel Collection.

32. Louise Ogawa to Miss Breed, September 27, 1942, accession no. 93.75.31N, Japanese American National Museum (gift of Elizabeth Yamada).

33. Lillie Y. McCabe, interview by Jeffrey B. Yamada, October 19, 1987, Nisei Experience, O.H. 1949, 2, 6, OHP-CSUF.

34. Kikuko Nakagiri Ishida, in *Blossoms in the Desert: Topaz High School Class of 1945,* ed. Darrell Y. Hamamoto (South San Francisco: Giant Horse Printing, 2003), 56.

35. McCabe, interview, 2.

36. Yoshie Mary Tashima, interview by Pat Tashima, February 15, 1974, Japanese American Evacuation, O.H. 1360, 5, OHP-CSUF.

37. Yasumitsu "Yas" Furuya, in Hamamoto, *Blossoms in the Desert,* 27–28.

38. "She Makes 'Em Herself," *Manzanar Free Press,* June 2, 1942, 4.

39. Oye, in Tsuchida, *Reflections,* 294. As Martha Inouye Oye remembered of her experiences at Minidoka: "Comfort was uppermost in the minds of the people when they first arrived here. As at the assembly centers, talented and creative evacuees built partitions and furniture from discarded lumber and material picked up around the barracks to make their rooms more habitable."

40. Okubo, *Citizen 13660*, 132, 137–138.

41. Egami, *Evacuation Diary*, 78.

42. Noboru Shirai, *Tule Lake: An Issei Memoir* (Sacramento: Muteki Press, 2001), 54–55.

43. Maye Mitsuye Oye Uemura, in Tsuchida, *Reflections*, 347; and Edith Watanabe, public testimony before the Commission on Wartime Relocation and Internment of Civilians, Seattle, September 9, 1981, reel 4, 217, National Archives and Records Administration.

44. Minoru Yasui, in Tsuchida, *Reflections*, 77.

45. Yukiko Furuta, interview by Arthur Hansen and Yasko Gamo, June 17 and July 6, 1982 Issei Experience in Orange County, CA, O.H. 1752, 39, Historical and Cultural Foundation of Orange County, Japanese American Council, and OHP-CSUF.

46. Uchida, *Desert Exile*, 78.

47. McCabe, interview, 2.

48. Kimi Yamada Yanari, in Tsuchida, *Reflections*, 162–163.

49. Egami, *Evacuation Diary*, 60; and Yuri Kochiyama, *Fishmerchant's Daughter: An Oral History* (New York: Community Documentation Workshop, 1981), 1:13. At Tulare, furniture crafters were described as "menfolk" who skillfully transformed discarded apples boxes and orange crates into couches, ironing boards, and tables; at Santa Anita, internees made furniture from cardboard cartoons.

50. June Igaue, interview by Nancy Aweimrine, November 12, 1984, Internment Experience in World War II, O.H. 1769, 9, OHP-CSUP.

51. "The Boom Town, Part III: A Day in the Relocation Center," YWCA Records, no. 025–18, box 50, folder 5, 47, Sophia Smith Collection, Smith College.

52. Noriko S. Bridges, written testimony to the Commission on Wartime Relocation and Internment of Civilians, San Francisco, August 11, 1981; also in U.S. Commission on Wartime Relocation and Internment of Civilians, *Personal Justice Denied: Report of the Commission on Wartime Relocation and Internment of Civilians*, ed. and with a foreword by Tetsuden Kashima (Seattle: University of Washington Press, 1997), 161.

53. Shuzo Chris Kato, testimony before the Commission on Wartime Relocation and Internment of Civilians, Seattle, September 9, 1981, reel 4, 201, National Archives and Records Administration.

54. Igaue, interview, 11.

55. Yanari, in Tsuchida, *Reflections*, 163.

56. Nomi, *Nisei Odyssey: The Camp Years* (Fountain Valley, CA: Bowder Publishing, 1991), 184.

57. Okubo, *Citizen 13660*, 137.

58. Kasen Noda, in *Internees: War Relocation Center Memoirs and Diaries*, ed. Takeo Kaneshiro (New York: Vintage Press, 1976), 15.

59. George Fukasawa, interview by Arthur Hansen, August 12, 1974, Japanese American Evacuation, O.H. 1336, OHP-CSUF; and Arthur A. Hansen, ed., *Japanese American World War II Evacuation Oral History Project, Part I: Internees* (Westport, CT: Meckler, 1991), 242,

60. Shiro Nomura, "Inside Manzanar during World War 2," *Inyo Museums News Bulletin*, February 1975, pt. 5, 3.

61. Shirai, *Tule Lake*, 54.

62. Kazutoshi Mayeda, testimony before the Commission on Wartime Relocation and Internment of Civilians, Chicago, September 22, 1981, reel 5, 220, National Archives and Records Administration.

63. "Taking Lumber without Proper Authority Banned," *Denson Tribune*, May 25, 1943, 1; Yuki, "Your Home and Mine," *Heart Mountain Sentinel*, November 14, 1942, 3.

64. Egami, *Evacuation Diary*, 60, 78; "From Cooking to Carpentry," 5.

65. Allen H. Eaton, *Beauty behind Barbed Wire: The Arts of the Japanese in Our War Relocation Camps* (New York: Harper and Brothers, 1952), 66–67.

66. Tami, "Women's Mirror: Cloth Giraffe," *Topaz Times*, January 16, 1943, 5; Tami, "Women's Mirror," *Topaz Times*, January 23, 1943, 5.

67. Tomoye Ta, "Women's Mirror: Pot-Holder," *Topaz Times*, February 27, 1943, 5.

68. Kumiko Ishida, in Hamamoto, *Blossoms in the Desert*, 60.

69. Tashima, interview, 5.

70. Kochiyama, *Fishmerchant's Daughter*, 13.

71. Uchida, *Desert Exile*, 78.

72. Sone, *Nisei Daughter*, 177, 196.

73. Ishigo, *Lone Heart Mountain*, 48; Eaton, *Beauty behind Barbed Wire*, 164–165.

74. Fusa Tsumagari to Clara Breed, November 23, 1942, accession no. 93.75.31IH, Japanese American National Museum.

75. Miwako Oana, "Scratch Pad," *Heart Mountain Sentinel*, February 6, 1942, 5.

76. Kudo Masanobu, *The History of Ikebana* (Tokyo: Shufunotomo, 1986); Patricia Massy, *The Essentials of Ikebana* (Tokyo: Shufunotomo, 1978).

77. Eaton, *Beauty behind Barbed Wire*, 22–23, 58–59.

78. Ibid., 82–83.

79. Ibid., 136–137.

80. Molly Miyako Kimura, interview by Hiroko Tsuda, February 2, 1995, Sacramento, Oral History Project of the Japanese American Citizens League (Florin chapter), and Oral History Program, California State University, Sacramento (OHP-CSUS).

81. Shigeno Hoka Nishimi, interview by Marion Kanemoto, September 22, 1992, Sacramento, Oral History Program of the Japanese American Citizens League (Florin chapter), and OHP-CSUS.

82. See examples of futoi at http://www.hana300.com/futoi (accessed March 21, 2008).

83. Fletcher Bowron to John Toland, April 27, 1942, in *Report by the U.S. House Select Committee Investigating National Defense Migration* (Tolan Committee report), 77th Cong., 2nd sess., 1942, H.R. 2124, ser. 10668, 40.

Private property owned by Japanese Americans was confiscated by both legal and illegal means. The assets of most Issei were frozen and controlled by a complicated and opaque web of bureaucracy created by the Federal Reserve Bank, the Farm Security Administration, and the Office of the Alien Property Custodian. To retain ownership of private property, Issei were required to complete inventory forms referred to as TRF-300, an obligation of which many were unaware. Property owned by Nisei was pilfered and stolen, with many Caucasians obtaining "legal" title through corrupt means. Regardless of the method used for the pilfering, the uncompensated economic losses of Japanese Americans equaled nearly $400 million in 1945 dollars, as estimated by the congressional Commission on Wartime Relocation and Internment of Civilians (CWRIC). When adjusted to 1985 standards, this amount was the equivalent of $2 billion. For more discussion of economic losses, see U.S. Commission on Wartime Relocation and Internment of Civilians, *Personal Justice Denied*, 60–61, 122, 131–132; Michi Nishiura Weglyn, *Years of Infamy: The Untold story of America's Concentration Camps* (Seattle: University of Washington Press, 1995), 76. Proceedings and Extension of Remarks, *Congressional Record*, December 12, 1985, 99th Cong., 1st sess.; Continuation of House Proceedings, *Congressional Record*, December 11, 1985, 99th Cong., 1st sess.; http://bss.sfsu.edu/internment/ Congressional%20Records/1985 (accessed March 21, 2008

84. Nishimi, interview.

85. Eaton, *Beauty behind Barbed Wire*, 68–69, 158–159.

86. "Artistic Talent Shown," *Denson Tribune*, March 2, 1943, 2; YO, "Tree Knobs Exhibit Opens," *Communique*, February 23, 1943, 3; Eaton, *Beauty behind Barbed Wire*, 10–11, 32–33, 106, 114.

87. Eaton, *Beauty behind Barbed Wire*, 16, 88–89.

88. Yoshito Wayne Osaki, "The Paper Christmas Tree," in Japanese Cultural and Community Center of Northern California, *From Our Side of the Fence*, 53.

89. Ishigo, *Lone Heart Mountain*, 23.

90. Okubo, *Citizen 13660*, 136.

91. Nomi, *Nisei Odyssey*, 52–53.

92. Kikuchi, *Kikuchi Diary*, 84.

93. Okubo, *Citizen 13660*, 83; Uchida, *Desert Exile*, 96.

94. Fusa Tsumagari to Clara Breed, July 16, 1942, accession no. 93.75.31JA, Japanese American National Museum.

95. Ueysugi, interview, 5, 7.

96. Jeffrey F. Burton, Mary M. Farrell, Florence B. Lord, and Richard W. Lord, eds., *Confinement and Ethnicity: An Overview of World War II Japanese American Relocation Sites* (Seattle: University of Washington Press, 2000), 101–128; U.S. Army, *Final Report, 1942*, 273.

97. Burton et al., *Confinement and Ethnicity*, 154.

98. John Hirohata, "Attractive Nameplates Adorn Center Apartments," *Denson Tribune*, March 12, 1943, 3.

99. Eaton, *Beauty behind Barbed Wire*, 26–27.

100. T.O., "Plain and Fancy Mailboxes Decorate Homes," *Communique*, February 16, 1943, 5.

101. Ishigo, *Lone Heart Mountain*, 48; and Eaton, *Beauty behind Barbed Wire*, 138–139.

102. Burton et al., *Confinement and Ethnicity*, 163.

103. "Resident Makes 1000 'Shakushi,'" *Heart Mountain Sentinel*, May 1, 1943, 8.

104. "Tanforan Tour," *Tanforan Totalizer*, June 27, 1942, 6; Eaton, *Beauty behind Barbed Wire*, 14–15.

105. "Ingenuity Used in Decorations," *Communique*, December 24, 1942, 2.

106. Ishigo, *Lone Heart Mountain*, 52.

107. Shiro Nomura, "Inside Manzanar during World War 2," *Inyo Museums News Bulletin*, December 1975, pt. 14C, 5.

108. Grace Morioka to Esther ___, Poston, AZ, September 10, YWCA Records, no. 025–18, box 50, folder 2, 2, Sophia Smith Collection.

109. Alice ___ to Kimi Mukaye, YWCA national secretary, Amache Young Women's Christian Association Hospitality House, April 13, 1943, YWCA I, box 49a, folder 2, 2, Sophia Smith Collection.

110. Winona Chambers, report of local visit, Gila Relocation Center, Rivers, AZ, May 9–14, 1944, YWCA I, box 49a, folder 1, 3, Sophia Smith Collection;

"Narrative Report for Quarter ending December 31, 1944, Canal Advisory Board, 2," Gila River Relocation Center, Rivers, AZ, YWCA I, box 49a, folder 1, Sophia Smith Collection.

111. Uchida, *Desert Exile*, 126.

112. Egami, *Evacuation Diary*, 89.

113. *Our Daily Diary*, May 26, 1943, MSS A 1031, Utah State Historical Society, Salt Lake City.

114. Sheryl Ritchie, "School Life in Poston," in *Through Innocent Eyes: Writings and Art from the Japanese American Internment by Poston I Schoolchildren*, ed. Vincent Tajiri (Los Angeles: Keiro Services Press, 1990), 46.

115. Hisako Watanabe to Clara Breed, January 7, 1943, accession no. 93.75.31JG, Japanese American National Museum.

116. Aiko Tanamachi Endo, interview by Marsha Bode, November 15, 1983, Nisei Experience in Orange County, CA, O.H. 1750, 34, Historical and Cultural Foundation of Orange County, Japanese American Council, and OHP-CSUF.

117. Igaue, interview, 10; Burton et al., *Confinement and Ethnicity*, 221–223; Alexander H. Leighton, *The Governing of Men: General Principles and Recommendations Based on Experience at a Japanese Relocation Camp* (New York: Octagon Books, 1964), 104.

118. Fusa Tsumagari to Clara Breed, October 9, 1942, accession no. 93.75.31FB, Japanese American National Museum.

119. John Hirohata, "Cabinet Shop Is One of the Busiest in Center," *Denson Tribune*, March 16, 1943, 3.

120. "Carpenter Shop Products Varied," *Denson Tribune*, April 9, 1943, 3.

121. Butte Community Quarterly Report, YWCA, October 1–December 31, 1944, YWCA I, box 49a, folder 1, 4, Sophia Smith Collection.

122. Igaue, interview, 8.

123. Oye, in Tsuchida, *Reflections*, 294.

CHAPTER 3 — RE-TERRITORIALIZING OUTSIDE SPACES

1. Rick Bonus, *Locating Filipino Americans: Ethnicity and the Cultural Politics of Space* (Philadelphia: Temple University Press, 2000), 4.

2. Akhil Gupta and James Ferguson, "Beyond 'Culture': Space, Identity, and the Politics of Difference," *Cultural Anthropology 7* (1992): 11.

3. Mary Tsukamoto, in *And Justice for All: An Oral History of the Japanese American Detention Camps*, ed. John Tateishi (Seattle: University of Washington Press, 2001), 12–14.

4. Hatsuye Egami, *The Evacuation Diary of Hatsuye Egami*, ed. Claire Gorfinkel (Pasadena, CA: Intentional Productions, 1996), 61–62.

5. Yuri Kochiyama, *Fishmerchant's Daughter: An Oral History* (New York: Community Documentation Workshop, 1981), 1:13.

6. Charles Kikuchi, *The Kikuchi Diary: Chronicle from an American Concentration Camp*, ed. John Modell (Urbana: University of Illinois Press, 1993), 132–133. "In the infield there is an interesting garden. It is laid out beautifully and has some fragrant flowers already blooming. Around it is a sort of bamboo-like fence and right in the middle on a post is one of those Japanese lanterns. The whole thing looks like old Japan. Some people just can't divorce themselves from Japan and cling to the old traditions and ways. The garden is an outward indication of this sentiment for Japan. The odds are that the builder of the garden is pro-Japan, although he may have built it for cultural reasons" (ibid.).

7. Ibid., 34, 53.

8. "Model Planes, Tins, Tubes, Gardens," *Tanforan Totalizer*, June 13, 1942, 4; Kikuchi, *Kikuchi Diary*, 203; Mine Okubo, *Citizen 13660* (Seattle: University of Washington Press, 1983), 97; Nay, "Tanforan Tour," *Tanforan Totalizer*, August 1, 1942, 8.

9. Nay, "Tanforan Tour," *Tanforan Totalizer*, August 15, 1942, 8. "Although we knew that Tanforan was only a temporary home, we all worked constantly to make the windswept racetrack a more attractive and pleasant place. Dozens of small vegetable and flower gardens flourished along the barracks and stables, and a corner of camp that once housed a junk pile was transformed into a colorful camp garden of stocks, sweetpeas, irises, zinnias, and marigolds. A group of talented men also made a miniature park with trees and a waterfall, creating a small lake complete with a wooden bridge, pier, and an island. It wasn't much, but it was one of the many efforts made to comfort eye and heart." Yoshiko Uchida, *Desert Exile: The Uprooting of a Japanese-American Family* (1982; repr., Seattle: University of Washington Press, 2000), 93–94.

10. "The Reviewing Stand," *Tanforan Totalizer*, June 20, 1942, 2.

11. "Center Scenic Spot: North Lake," *Tanforan Totalizer*, August 5, 1942, 4; "Lake Opening," *Tanforan Totalizer*, August 1, 1942, 2.

12. Okubo, *Citizen 13660*, 98–99; "Tanforan Calendar," *Tanforan Totalizer*, September 12, 1942, n.p. (appears under August heading).

13. "Regatta," *Tanforan Totalizer*, July 11, 1942, 9.

14. "Tanforan's Sail Fleet," *Tanforan Totalizer*, June 27, 1942, 7.

15. Kikuchi, *Kikuchi Diary*, 2, 135.

16. In camp newspapers, published diaries, and War Relocation Authority photographs, images emerge of lonely, isolated, and powerless old men whiling away the hours by carving nameplates, model boats, and canes. Rather than framing model shipbuilding and the subsequent sailing activities of Issei men

at Lake Tanforan as vital elements of place making, Charles Kikuchi observed: "The Issei haven't anything else to do and I see them around all day long painstakingly carving out these boats" (ibid., 135). In a 1943 *Trek* article reporting on conditions at Poston, this image of emasculated Issei men was even more pronounced. "In many cases, once respected heads of families have been reduced to the status of futile old men, who spend their leisure hours cackling over choice bits of gossip, or polishing ironwood to wow the customers at the next Art and Hobby show, in the hope of perhaps regaining a part of their lost prestige." Jim Yamada, "Report from Poston," *Trek*, June 1943, 36. Another internee remembered a cane that her father carved and polished as a "sad, homemade version of the samurai sword his great-great-grandfather carried in the land around Hiroshima, at a time when such warriors weren't much needed anymore." Jeanne Wakatsuki Houston and James D. Houston, *Farewell to Manzanar* (New York: Bantam Books, 1973), 40.

A more subtle and especially revealing representation appeared in the *Camp Harmony Newsletter*, in which a fifty-four-year-old grandfather and prolific wood-carver was described as a compliant, "unpretentious little man." As the article reported to those imprisoned at Puyallup, Washington: "The thermometer may rise to 110 degrees, and the rains may beat down in furious assault, but there is one man who never complains. He sits whittling on a slab of rough thick bark—a picture of quiet contentment." Beyond his role as a grandfather, the carver is also identified as a former agricultural worker, with the internee reporter informing readers that "the carefully tended acres of lettuce and peas and berries are no longer his immediate environs." Tadako Tamaura, "Okitsu Pride of 'C' Carvers Has Made Hobby into Art," *Camp Harmony Newsletter*, July 10, 1942, 3. Here we are offered an image of a man sitting alone, devoid of community, occupation, and role as family patriarch. No mention is made of the product of his activity or the contribution his work made to improving camp life. Even the functional craft activity of furniture making was sometimes portrayed negatively. Commenting on the vast array of furniture made by men imprisoned at Tulare, Hatsuye Egami observed: "The creator of each piece looks upon each finished product with a sense of pride. But when I realize that these bits of salvaged wood are shaped into such pieces partly to while away the idle hours, I am overtaken with sadness" (*Evacuation Diary*, 60).

17. Gary Okihiro, "The Japanese in America," in *Encyclopedia of Japanese American History: An A–Z Reference from 1868 to the Present*, ed. Brian Niiya (New York: Checkmark Books, 2001), 15.

18. Kikuchi, *Kikuchi Diary*, 203; "Center Garden," *Tanforan Totalizer*, July 11, 1942, 4; "Garden Exhibit," *Tanforan Totalizer*, August 22, 1942, 3.

19. Uchida, *Desert Exile*, 93–94.

20. Ibid., 100.

21. Miyuki Aoyama, "Flower Garden Adds Color to Center," *Santa Anita Pacemaker*, May 26, 1942, 3.

22. Fred Yamamoto, "Ingenuity Produces Unique Center Rock Garden," *Santa Anita Pacemaker*, July 15, 1942, 4; Aoyama, "Flower Garden Adds Color," 3.

23. Miyuki Aoyama, "Tin Cans Used," *Santa Anita Pacemaker*, July 18, 1942, 2.

24. Eddie Shimano, "Who's Zoo," *Santa Anita Pacemaker*, July 4, 1942, 6; Miyuki Aoyama. "Spruce Use of Wood Good: Creation Is Sensation," *Santa Anita Pacemaker*, June 27, 1942, 4.

25. "First Harvesting at Santa Anita," *Manzanar Free Press*, July 24, 1942, 2; "We'll Grow 'Em and Eat 'Em," *Santa Anita Pacemaker*, July 1, 1942, 2; Anna Sakaizawa, "Center Radishes," *Santa Anita Pacemaker*, July 15, 1942, 2; "First Crops Harvested," *Santa Anita Pacemaker*, July 18, 1942, 2.

26. Scott Wong, "Rhyme of Her Life: Local Poet, Survivor of Japanese Internment Camp, Turns 100," *Los Altos Town Crier*, December 18, 2002, 1.

27. Kitty Nakagawa, Jean Kariya, and Mari Eijima, interviews by Sandra Taylor, June 14, 1988, Leonia, NJ, acc. 1002, box 3, folder 16, 21, Topaz Oral Histories, Special Collections, University of Utah Marriott Library. "My first perception was one of bleakness, that there was just black nothingness and dryness and I guess you might call it death, and little by little life began to appear as they imported those boxes of shrubs, you remember they were planting all over, and then little by little some semblance of life began to resume" (ibid.).

28. Hiromoto Katayama, interview by Sandra Taylor, October 27, 1987, Berkeley, CA, acc. 1002, box 2, folder 3, 28, Topaz Oral Histories; Iijima Kazu, interview by Sandra Taylor, October 6, 1986, New York City, acc. 1002, box 2, folder 1, 6, Topaz Oral Histories; Minoru Kiyota, *Beyond Loyalty: The Story of a Kibei*, trans. Linda Klepinger Keenan (Honolulu: University of Hawai'i Press, 1997), 76; Okubo, *Citizen 13660*, 192–193, 149–150.

29. "Our Daily Diary," May 28, 1943, MSS A 1031, Utah State Historical Society, Salt Lake City.

30. Leonard J. Arrington, *The Price of Prejudice: The Japanese American Relocation Center in Utah during World War II* (1962; repr., Delta, UT: Topaz Museum, 1997), 24, 25, 37.

31. Uchida, *Desert Exile*, 138.

32. Yoshie Mary Tashima, interview by Pat Tashima, February 15, 1974, Japanese American Evacuation, O.H. 1360, 5, Oral History Program, Japanese American Project, California State University, Fullerton (OHP-CSUF). "There

weren't any trees, or shrubs, or greenery—just barracks out in the middle of the desert and a great, big wire fence around there so we wouldn't escape. . . . We finally landscaped that desert into something beautiful. It's just remarkable what people can do to a nothing place. We planted trees, flowers, and a lawn."

33. Mas Ueysugi, interview by John McFarlane, April 16, 1971, Japanese American Evacuation, O.H. 1071, 7, OHP-CSUF.

34. Mas Tanibata, interview by Mary Tamura, March 4, 1994, 10, Terminal Island Life History Project, Japanese American National Museum, Los Angeles.

35. Tom Watanabe, in Tateishi, *Justice for All*, 94–99.

36. Roy Nash, "From the Project Director Roy Nash," *Manzanar Free Press*, July 27, 1942, 2.

37. Caleb Foote, "Outcasts!" in *The Lost Years: 1942–1946*, ed. Sue Kunitomi Embrey (Los Angeles: Moonlight Publications, 1972), 40.

38. Anonymous, interview by Richard Curtiss, March 4, 1966, Japanese American Evacuation, O.H. 11, 17, OHP-CSUF. "Oh yes, the people planted shrubbery and improved the place to make it more livable. It got better all the time. When we first went there, it was dusty and nothing there" (ibid.).

39. As part of the deal, the WRA agreed to develop agricultural land and build roads.

40. Jeffrey F. Burton, Mary M. Farrell, Florence B. Lord, and Richard W. Lord, eds., *Confinement and Ethnicity: An Overview of World War II Japanese American Relocation Sites* (Seattle: University of Washington Press, 2000), 61.

41. U.S. Commission on Wartime Relocation and Internment of Civilians, *Personal Justice Denied: Report of the Commission on Wartime Relocation and Internment of Civilians*, ed. and with a foreword by Tetsuden Kashima (Seattle: University of Washington Press, 1997), 168.

42. Paul Vokota, "At Random: Victory Gardens," *Denson Tribune*, April 16, 1943, 2.

43. Paul Vokota, "At Random: Green Lawn," *Denson Tribune*, March 30, 1943, 2; and "'Green Lawn' Turns Out to Be Chives," *Denson Tribune*, April 2, 1943, 2.

44. "Variety of Plants Sold at Center Stores," *Denson Tribune*, March 12, 1943, 4.

45. Allen H. Eaton, *Beauty behind Barbed Wire: The Arts of the Japanese in Our War Relocation Camps* (New York: Harper and Brothers, 1952), 50–51, 160–161.

46. "Tin Cans Used by Resident for Victory Garden," *Heart Mountain Sentinel*, March 27, 1943, 8.

47. Estelle Ishigo, *Lone Heart Mountain* (Los Angeles: Anderson, Ritchie, and Simon, 1972), 47–48, 50, 62.

48. Katsu Oikawa, "Combined Victory Garden Grows under Heart Mountain Shadow," *Heart Mountain Sentinel*, July 3, 1943, 8.

49. "Actual Work on Hotbeds Begun," *Heart Mountain Sentinel*, March 27, 1943, 8.

50. "Topsoil," *Heart Mountain Sentinel*, April 17, 1943, 5. Ed Tokeshi, "2000 Acre Victory Garden Rises in Midst of Desert," *Heart Mountain Sentinel*, May 8, 1943, 5.

51. *Random House Unabridged Dictionary* (New York: Random House, 1997), at Infoplease, http://www.infoplease.com (accessed March 22, 2008).

52. Ed Tokeshi, "West Coast Pioneers Toil on Virgin Land," *Heart Mountain Sentinel*, May 8, 1943, 5.

53. "Local Farm Program Is Speeded," *Heart Mountain Sentinel*, June 26, 1943, 8; Ishigo, *Lone Heart Mountain*, 76.

54. "Caravan on Way North; Autos Piled High with Goods," *Los Angeles Daily News*, March 23, 1942, 1, 8.

55. "1000 Japs Leave L.A. by Car, Train as Big Exodus On," *Los Angeles Daily News*, March 23, 1942, 1.

56. Jeff Putman and Genny Smith, eds., *Deepest Valley: Guide to Owens Valley* (Reno: University of Nevada Press, 1995), 254; and Phil Garrison, "Evacuees Challenged to Equal Valley Pioneers," *Los Angeles Daily News*, March 25, 1942, 3, 17.

57. Putman and Smith, *Deepest Valley*, 256.

58. Jeffrey F. Burton, *Three Farewells to Manzanar: The Archeology of Manzanar National Historic Site*, Publications in Anthropology 67 (Tucson: Western Archeological and Conservation Center, National Park Service, U.S. Department of the Interior, 1996), 1:3.

59. "Planning a Lawn?" *Manzanar Free Press*, July 7, 1942, 4. Internees planting lawns at Manzanar were able to borrow rakes and shovels, and obtain seed from block leaders.

60. "Gardens: Harvest Time to Be Here Soon," *Manzanar Free Press*, June 9, 1942, 4.

61. Sue Kunitomi Embrey, Arthur A. Hansen, and Betty Kulberg Mitson, eds., *Manzanar Martyr: An Interview with Harry Y. Ueno* (Anaheim, CA: Shumway Family Historical Series, 1986), 28–30.

62. "Harvest Time Near for Local Farms," *Manzanar Free Press*, July 4, 1942, 3.

63. "Watermelon Seeds Planted" and "125 Acres Cultivated," *Manzanar Free Press*, June 4, 1942, 3.

64. Shiro Nomura, "Inside Manzanar during World War 2," *Inyo Museums News Bulletin*, April 1975, pt. 7, 3; "Harvest Time Near for Local Farms," 3.

65. "Harvesting of Pears from Orchard Begins," *Manzanar Free Press,* August 26, 1942, 1.

66. Shiro Nomura, "Inside Manzanar during World War 2," *Inyo Museums News Bulletin,* May 1975, pt. 8, 7, and June 1975, pt. 9, 6.

67. Houston and Houston, *Farewell to Manzanar,* 85–87.

68. Ibid., 95.

69. "Children's Village," *Manzanar Free Press,* July 7, 1942, 4.

70. Takatow Matsuno, interview by Noemi Romero, March 13, 1993, Japanese American Experience, O.H. 1080, 17, OHP-CSUF; and Lisa N. Nobe, "The Children's Village at Manzanar: The World War II Eviction and Detention of Japanese American Orphans," *Journal of the West* 38, no. 2 (April 1999): 65–71.

71. "Tule Produce Arrives Here," *Poston Chronicle,* December 16, 1943, 2; Noboru Shirai, *Tule Lake: An Issei Memoir* (Sacramento, CA: Muteki Press, 2001), 116.

72. Esther Briesemeister, "America's Children: What Happened to Us," Japanese Evacuee Project Report, September 1946, YWCA Records, no. 025–18, box 9, folder 18, 8, Sophia Smith Collection, Smith College.

73. John Bird, "Our Japs Have Gone to Work," *Country Gentlemen,* August 1942, 7.

74. "Relocation Camps Will Close as Disloyal Japs Are Interned and Others Take Jobs," *St. Joseph News-Press,* July 194?, contained in YWCA Records, no. 025–18, box 221, folder SB3, 84, Sophia Smith Collection.

75. "Japanese-American Evacuees Not Mistreated nor Pampered," *Monitor,* July 16, 1943, 3.

76. Tanibata, interview, 8. Kikuchi, *Kikuchi Diary,* 203.

77. "Reviewing Stand," 2.

78. "Divotmakers' Delight," *Tanforan Totalizer,* August 1, 1942, 4.

79. "Open Golf Tourney in 'A' Sun," *Camp Harmony Newsletter,* July 18, 1942, 6; "Golf Course Opens in 'A,'" *Camp Harmony Newsletter,* July 10, 1942, 4.

80. Elaine S. Okimoto, interview by Betty E. Mitson, April 4, 1972, Japanese American Experience, O.H. 1080, 13, OHP-CSUF; "The Compass: Poston Chronicle," *Denson Tribune,* March 2, 1943, 2; "Unit III Swimming Pool Is Not Officially Opened to Public," *Poston Chronicle,* April 20, 1944, 2; "Swimming Pool Opens," *Poston Chronicle: Poston III,* July 2, 1944.

81. Ishigo, *Lone Heart Mountain,* 78.

82. Burton et al., *Confinement and Ethnicity,* 205.

83. *Camp Harmony Newsletter* (special souvenir ed.), August 14, 1942; unidentified Japanese American woman, interview by Anne O. Freed, April 17, 1943, reel 1, War Relocation Authority records, Puyallup Assembly Center, 1942–1946,

Field Basic Documentation, National Archives, Washington, DC. Also online at http://www.lib.washington.edu/exhibits/harmony/Documents (accessed March 22, 2008).

84. "New workers and apprentices" were paid $12 a month for WRA-sponsored jobs; "common labor requiring hard physical work" was valued at $16 a month; and internees in jobs "requiring responsible supervision, professional training, and exceptional skills received $19 a month (Ishigo, *Lone Heart Mountain*, 24, 78). *Sears, Roebuck and Company Catalogue*, Fall/Winter 1942, 887. Stanley Hayami, diary (1941–1944), 36r, Japanese American National Museum (gift from the estate of Frank Naoichi and Asano Hayami, parents of Stanley Kunio Hayami).

85. Hayami, diary (1941–1944), 19v, 22r, 23v, 64r.

86. Miwako Oana, "Scratch Pad," *Heart Mountain Sentinel*, February 6, 1943, 5.

87. Kumiko Kariya Matsumoto, in *Blossoms in the Desert: Topaz High School Class of 1945*, ed. Darrell Y. Hamamoto (South San Francisco: Giant Horse Printing, 2003), 125; Okubo, *Citizen 13660*, 158; "Landscapists Stake Out Rink," *Topaz Times*, December 5, 1942, 20. Uchida, *Desert Exile*, 122, 124, 128.

88. John Hirohata, "Spring Comes to Denson," *Denson Tribune*, April 6, 1943, 2; H.K., "Where 2000 Baseball Fans Came to See Opener," *Denson Tribune*, May 14, 1943, 7; Shiro Nomura, "Inside Manzanar during World War 2," *Inyo Museums News Bulletin*, August 1975, pt. 10B, 9; "Softball Diamonds Ready," *Heart Mountain Sentinel* (suppl.), General Information Bulletin, series 10, September 14, 1942, 4.

89. "Three Youthful Basketball Fans Invent Miniature Cage Game," *Santa Anita Pacemaker*, June 2, 1942, 2.

90. Kikuchi, *Kikuchi Diary*, 73.

91. Monica Sone, *Nisei Daughter* (Seattle: University of Washington Press, 2000), 173.

92. Okubo, *Citizen 13660*, 33–35, 161.

93. Hiromoto Katayama, Fumi Hayashi, and Eiko Hosei Katayama, interview by Sandra Taylor, October 27, 1987, Berkeley, CA, acc. 1002, box 2, folder 3, 56, Topaz Oral Histories.

94. Okubo, *Citizen 13660*, 148.

95. Russell Bearden, "Life inside Arkansas's Japanese-American Relocation Centers," *Arkansas Historical Quarterly* 48, no. 2, (1989): 169–196.

96. "Women Work on Landscaping Job," *Communique*, November 22, 1942, 1.

97. Uchida, *Desert Exile*, 109.

98. "If Mud Sticks to Your Shoes, It's Good," *Communique*, December 11, 1942, 4.

99. "Evacuees Produce Own Vegetables," *Topaz Times,* April 1, 1944, 1.

100. H.K., "Popular Place in Block 17," *Denson Tribune,* May 14, 1943, 3.

101. "Arbors Must Be Removed," *Denson Tribune,* May 21, 1943, 1.

CHAPTER 4 — MAKING CONNECTIONS

1. My critique of community is heavily influenced by Miranda Joseph's work, especially *Against the Romance of Community* (Minneapolis: University of Minnesota Press, 2002).

2. Charles Kikuchi, *The Kikuchi Diary: Chronicle from an American Concentration Camp,* ed. John Modell (Urbana: University of Illinois Press, 1993), 10–11, 62.

3. Ibid., 116, 236.

4. Allen H. Eaton, *Beauty behind Barbed Wire: The Arts of the Japanese in Our War Relocation Camps* (New York: Harper and Brothers, 1952), 98–99.

5. June Igaue, interview by Nancy Aweimrine, November 12, 1984, Internment Experience in World War II, O.H. 1769, 8, Oral History Program, Japanese American Project, California State University, Fullerton (OHP-CSUF); and Elaine S. Okimoto, interview by Betty E. Mitson, April 4, 1972, Japanese American Experience, O.H. 1080, 13, OHP-CSUF.

6. Kikuchi, *Kikuchi Diary,* 241.

7. Mine Okubo, *Citizen 13660* (Seattle: University of Washington Press, 2002), 104.

8. Katherine Tasaki to Helen McNary, March 5, 1943, accession no. 93.75.31AJ, Japanese American National Museum, Los Angeles. Photograph by Dorothea Lange, June 30, 1942, WRA no. C-901, Manzanar, NARA Record Group 210-G-10C-901, National Archives and Records Administration, College Park, MD. Lillie Y. McCabe, interview by Jeffrey B. Yamada, October 19, 1987, Nisei Experience, O.H. 1949, 18, OHP-CSUF.

9. Fusa Tsumagari to Clara Breed, August 20, 1942, accession no. 93.75.31JB, Japanese American National Museum.

10. Kikuchi, *Kikuchi Diary,* 217.

11. Yoshiko Uchida, *Desert Exile: The Uprooting of a Japanese-American Family* (1982; repr., Seattle: University of Washington Press, 2000), 78.

12. Fumi Hayashi, interview by Sandra Taylor, October 28, 1987, Berkeley, CA, acc. 1002, box 3, folder 11, 8, Topaz Oral Histories, Special Collections, University of Utah Marriott Library.

13. Seiko Akahoshi and Baba Brodbeck, in *Blossoms in the Desert: Topaz High School Class of 1945,* ed. Darrell Y. Hamamoto (South San Francisco: Giant Horse Printing, 2003), 15–16.

14. Daisy Uyeda Satoda, in *From Our Side of the Fence: Growing Up in America's Concentration Camps,* by Japanese Cultural and Community Center of Northern California, ed. Brian Komei Dempster (San Francisco: Kearny Street Workshop Press, 2001), 69.

15. Katsumi Kunitsugu, interview by Sherry Turner, July 15, 1973, Nisei Experience, O.H. 1333, 12, OHP-CSUF.

16. Tosie Kusama, Rohwer autobiography no. 43, English 11-A, period 5, December 17, 1942, Gould/Vogel Collection, McGehee, AR.

17. Fusa Tsumagari to Clara Breed, October 9, 1942, accession no. 93.75.31FB, Japanese American National Museum.

18. Stanley Hayami, diary (1941–1944), 25r, Japanese American National Museum (gift from the estate of Frank Naoichi and Asano Hayami, parents of Stanley Kunio Hayami).

19. Noboru Shirai, *Tule Lake: An Issei Memoir* (Sacramento, CA: Muteki Press, 2001), 146.

20. Bill Hosokawa, *Nisei: The Quiet Americans* (New York: William Morrow, 1969), 377–378.

21. Dorothy S. Harada Oda, in Hamamoto, *Blossoms in the Desert,* 170.

22. Seiko Akahoshi and Baba Brodbeck, in Hamamoto, *Blossoms in the Desert,* 14.

23. Shirai, *Tule Lake,* 145.

24. "Food Committee Awaits Suggestions," *Santa Anita Pacemaker,* May 26, 1942, 3; "Menu," *Topaz Times,* December 24, 1942, 2; "New Mess System to Start Monday," *Santa Anita Pacemaker,* July 18, 1942, 1; "Mess System Reorganized," *Manzanar Free Press,* July 18, 1942, 1; "Mess: Greatest Feeding Problem of Evacuation Movement," *Santa Anita Pacemaker* (final and souvenir ed.), 10; "New Work, Meal Sked Will Begin Monday," *Topaz Times,* April 8, 1944, 1.

25. Okubo, *Citizen 13660,* 89.

26. Toyo Suyemoto, "Another Spring," in *Last Witnesses: Reflections on the Wartime Internment of Japanese Americans,* ed. Erica Harth (New York: Palgrave, 2001), 22.

27. Shiro Nomura, "Inside Manzanar during World War 2," *Inyo Museums News Bulletin,* April 1976, pt. 18C, 4.

28. Fumiko Fukuyama to Eddie ___, Santa Anita, June 14, 1942, YWCA Records, no. 025–18, box 48, folder 2, Sophia Smith Collection, Smith College.

29. Kikuchi, *Kikuchi Diary,* 62, 90, 122, 182, 225.

30. Nobuko Hanzawa, Rohwer autobiography no. 135, English 4, period 2, December 1942, Gould/Vogel Collection.

31. Asami Kawachi, "Feminine Forum," *Santa Anita Pacemaker*, July 8, 1942, 3; "The Finishing Line," *Camp Harmony Newsletter*, July 10, 1942, 3.

32. "Tailoring Project Opens," *Communique*, November 20, 1942, 4; "Sewing Project Moved to 36–1, *Communique*, December 4, 1942, 3.

33. "Sewing Orders Will Not Be Accepted," *Communique*, February 2, 1943, 6.

34. "Alterations Department Kept Busy," *Denson Tribune*, April 13, 1943, 2; "Sewing Machines Placed in Each Block," *Denson Tribune*, May 25, 1943, 4; Paul Yokota, "At Random: Sewing Machines," *Denson Tribune*, April 9, 1943, 2.

35. Jeanne Wakatsuki Houston and James D. Houston, *Farewell to Manzanar* (New York: Bantam Books, 1973), 29; Shiro Nomura and Mary Nomura, interview by Cathryn Piercy, October 10 and 11, 1973, 4–5, O.H. 32.2, Eastern California Museum, Independence, CA.

36. "Shower Curtains Promised," *Manzanar Free Press*, June 13, 1942, 4.

37. Hatsuye Egami, *The Evacuation Diary of Hatsuye Egami*, ed. Claire Gorfinkel (Pasadena, CA: Intentional Productions, 1996), 45–46.

38. Shiro Nomura, "Inside Manzanar during World War 2," *Inyo Museums News Bulletin*, April 1975, pt. 7, 3, 4.

39. Mrs. Mary Tsukamoto to Miss Briesemeister, Denver YWCA, May 4, 1943, YWCA 1, box 49A, folder 4: Jerome, 3, Sophia Smith Collection.

40. "Embroidery Exhibit in Powell Proves Big Hit," *Heart Mountain Sentinel*, January 9, 1943, 2; "Embroidery Class Meets at 17–26-S," *Heart Mountain Sentinel*, December 11, 1943, 8.

41. Roy Nakata to Alice Sinclair Dodge, July 30, 1942, box 1, Correspondence 1942–1946 file, Alice Sinclair Dodge Collection, Hoover Institution, Stanford University.

42. Kei Ichihashi to Mrs. Treat, August 1, 1943, in *Morning Glory, Evening Shadow: Yamato Ichihashi and His Internment Writings, 1942–1945*, ed., annotated, and with a biographical essay by Gordon H. Chang (Stanford: Stanford University Press, 1997), 245.

43. Margaret Ishino to Clara Breed, May 15, 1942, accession no. 93.75.31 GZ, Japanese American National Museum.

44. Margaret Ishino to Clara Breed, October 19, 1942, accession no. 93.75.31 CQ, Japanese American National Museum.

45. "Knitting Exhibit Scheduled," *Poston Chronicle: Poston III*, May 11, 1944, 3.

46. "Exhibit to Hold Furniture Sale," *Manzanar Free Press*, January 1, 1943, 1; "Carpentry Class to Hold First Annual Exhibit," *Manzanar Free Press*, January 6, 1943, 3.

47. Kotono Kato, interview by Mary Tsukamoto, May 3 and 10, 1989, Sacramento, CA, Oral History Project of the Japanese American Citizens League (Florin chapter) and Oral History Program, California State University, Sacramento.

48. "Pupils to Display Work in Flowers," *Heart Mountain Sentinel*, June 12, 1943, 3.

49. "Flower Classes Display Talent," *Denson Tribune*, May 21, 1943, 5.

50. T.O., "Beauty Is Not Only Bark Deep," *Communique*, January 26, 1943, 3.

51. Jeffrey F. Burton, Mary M. Farrell, Florence B. Lord, and Richard W. Lord, eds., *Confinement and Ethnicity: An Overview of World War II Japanese American Relocation Sites* (Seattle: University of Washington Press, 2000), 150; "Wood Carving Fans," *Communique*, November 13, 1942.

52. YO, "Tree Knobs Exhibit Opens," *Communique*, February 23, 1943, 3.

53. "Artistic Talent Shown," *Denson Tribune*, March 2, 1943, 2.

54. "Another Kobu Show Opens," *Denson Tribune*, March 16, 1943, 6.

55. "Arts Exhibit," *Communique*, December 31, 1942, 2.

56. "Three Life Sized Busts Featured in Conference Exhibit," *Communique*, November 17, 1942, 3.

57. "Kobu Exhibit," *Denson Tribune*, April 18, 1943, 6.

58. "Midget Violin Features Exhibit," *Denson Tribune*, March 9, 1943, 1; "Kobu Show Scheduled," *Denson Tribune*, March 5, 1943, 6.

59. "Art Students League Draws Large Crowd to Exhibit," *Heart Mountain Sentinel*, December 19, 1942, 8.

60. "Display of Art Works Slated," *Manzanar Free Press*, August 12, 1942, 3.

61. "Denson High School to Hold Open House Tonight," *Denson Tribune*, April 30, 1943, 1; "Open House Draws 2000," *Denson Tribune*, May 4, 1943, 1.

62. "2000 Attend School Exhibit," *Heart Mountain Sentinel*," August 28, 1943, 6.

63. Egami, *Evacuation Diary*, 79.

64. Miyuki Aoyama, "Creativeness Shown in Handicraft Exhibit," *Santa Anita Pacemaker*, July 4, 1942, 4; "Handicraft to Be Shown at Funita," *Santa Anita Pacemaker*, June 27, 1942, 3.

65. "Handicraft Show a Hit," *Santa Anita Pacemaker*, June 9, 1942, 1, 3.

66. "Director England to Open Handicraft Show," *Santa Anita Pacemaker*, June 6, 1942, 2.

67. "Art Exhibit Draws Crowd," *Manzanar Free Press*, June 2, 1942, 4.

68. "Visual Education Department Sponsors Exhibit until Saturday," *Manzanar Free Press*, December 25, 1942, 5.

69. "Museum in 'Hand-Made' Exhibit," *Manzanar Free Press,* January 6, 1943, 3.

70. "Art Exhibit Attracting Crowd," *Manzanar Free Press,* January 27, 1943, 1.

71. "Visual Education Museum in Exhibit," *Manzanar Free Press,* February 3, 1943, 2; "Art Exhibit in Block 2 Office," *Manzanar Free Press,* August 5, 1942, 2. Block 2's office at Manzanar was the site of an exhibit featuring eighty pieces of art ranging from posters to wood etchings and pencil sketches.

72. "Handicraft Exhibit Scheduled for May 20–21 at Auditorium," *Poston Chronicle: Poston 1,* May 16, 1944, 2; "Exhibit Today," *Poston Chronicle,* May 20, 1944, 1; "Thousands Jam Exhibit," *Poston Chronicle,* May 25, 1944, 1.

73. "Kobu Entries Still Taken," *Denson Tribune,* April 13, 1943, 1; "Throngs View Kobu," *Denson Tribune,* April 23, 1943, 1; "Takesako Chest Entry Wins 'Kobu' Show Prize," *Denson Tribune,* April 27, 1943, 1.

74. "Handicraft Show Planned," *Denson Tribune,* April 20, 1943, 6; "Handicraft Show Slated," *Denson Tribune,* April 27, 1943, 8; "Handicraft Show to Start Here Friday," *Denson Tribune,* May 4, 1943, 1; "Denson Fujin Kai Handicraft Exhibit Acclaimed Success," *Denson Tribune,* May 14, 1943, 6.

75. Uchida, *Desert Exile,* 87; "Garden Exhibit," *Tanforan Totalizer,* August 22, 1942, 3; "Mardi Gras Set for Labor Day Weekend," *Tanforan Totalizer,* August 29, 1942, 2; "Art and Hobby," *Tanforan Totalizer,* July 11, 1942, 4; Kimi Kodani Hill, *Topaz Moon: Chiura Obata's Art of the Internment* (Berkeley: Heyday Books, 2000), 45–46.

76. Estelle Ishigo, *Lone Heart Mountain* (Los Angeles: Anderson, Ritchie, and Simon, 1972), 71–72.

77. "Poster Shop Gets Thank You Letter," *Heart Mountain Sentinel,* August 14, 1943, 8.

78. Kasen Noda, in *Internees: War Relocation Center Memoirs and Diaries,* ed. Takeo Kaneshiro (New York: Vintage Press, 1976), 14.

79. "Flower Arrangement Classes Announced," *Heart Mountain Sentinel* (suppl.), General Information Bulletin, ser. 9, September 11, 1942, 2.

80. "Fashion Classes to Start Monday," *Heart Mountain Sentinel* (suppl.), General Information Bulletin, ser. 18, September 26, 1942, 2.

81. "Handicraft Classes Set," *Heart Mountain Sentinel,* October 31, 1942, 3.

82. "Ceramics Designer to Speak Tonight," *Heart Mountain Sentinel* (suppl.), General Information Bulletin, ser. 19, September 29, 1942, 3; "300 Hear Rhodes at Ceramics Meeting," *Heart Mountain Sentinel* (suppl.), General Information Bulletin, ser. 20, October 1, 1942, 5; "Equipment Due Here December," *Heart Mountain Sentinel,* November 7, 1942, 1; "Test Kiln Anticipated for Project,"

Heart Mountain Sentinel, January 1, 1943, 16; "Ceramics Shop Makes Ash Trays, Tea Cups," *Heart Mountain Sentinel,* May 29, 1943, 8.

83. "Enrollment Open for Art Classes," *Tanforan Totalizer,* May 15, 1942, 2; "Art Program Initiated," *Tanforan Totalizer,* May 30, 1942, 2; Hill, *Topaz Moon,* 46.

84. Hiyuki Aoyama, "Former Studio Artist Now Supervises Art Classes," *Santa Anita Pacemaker,* July 1, 1942, 3; "Art Classes," *Santa Anita Pacemaker,* June 6, 1942, 1; "Art Classes," *Santa Anita Pacemaker,* July 8, 1942, 3.

85. Asami Kawachi, "Feminine Forum," *Santa Anita Pacemaker,* July 15, 1942, 3; "Handicraft Classes Open," *Santa Anita Pacemaker,* May 1, 1942, 3.

86. Mary Tsukamoto, in *Justice for All: An Oral History of the Japanese American Detention Camps,* ed. John Tateshi (New York: Random House, 1984), 13.

87. Chang, *Ichihashi and His Internment Writings,* 234–245.

88. "Varied Art Classes Offered," *Manzanar Free Press,* June 27, 1942, 4.

89. "What's Knittin' Kitten?" *Manzanar Free Press,* June 13, 1942, 4; "For Men Only," *Manzanar Free Press,* June 27, 1942, 4; "Miladies Flock to Classes Daily," *Manzanar Free Press,* August 17, 1942, 3.

90. "Art Center Opens," *Manzanar Free Press,* June 6, 1942, 3.

91. Uchida, *Desert Exile,* 96–97.

CHAPTER 5 — MENTAL LANDSCAPES OF SURVIVAL

1. Some examples of mental illness include a mother who suffered a nervous breakdown, reel 3, August 11, 272, Linda Morimoto, Los Angeles, August 6, 1981, 104, found in U.S. Commission on Wartime Relocation and Internment of Civilians, *Personal Justice Denied: Report of the Commission on Wartime Relocation and Internment of Civilians,* ed. and with a foreword by Tetsuden Kashima (Seattle: University of Washington Press, 1997), 408. Another example is that of Mary Sugitachi, public testimony before the Commission on Wartime Relocation and Internment of Civilians, San Francisco, August 12, 1981, reel 3, 218, housed in the National Archives and Records Administration, College Park, MD.

2. Lillie Y. McCabe, interview by Jeffrey B. Yamada, October 19, 1987, Nisei Experience, O.H. 1949, 7, 13, 16, Oral History Program, Japanese American Project, California State University, Fullerton (OHP-CSUF).

3. Sugitachi, public testimony, 218.

4. Unidentified Japanese American woman, interview by Anne O. Freed, April 17, 1943, War Relocation Authority records, Puyallup Assembly Center, 1942–1946, Field Basic Documentation, National Archives, Washington, DC. Also online at http://www.lib.washington.edu/exhibits/harmony/Documents.

5. Mabel Ota, in *And Justice for All: An Oral History of the Japanese American Detention Camps*, ed. John Tateishi (Seattle: University of Washington Press, 1984), 111.

6. Helen Murao, in Tateishi, *Justice for All*, 44.

7. Hanaye Matsushita, in Louis Fiset, *Imprisoned Apart: The World War II Correspondence of an Issei Couple* (Seattle: University of Washington Press, 1997), 168.

8. Carey McWilliams, *Prejudice: Japanese Americans: Symbol of Racial Intolerance* (Boston: Little, Brown, 1944), 133. Also Michi Nishiura Weglyn, *Years of Infamy: The Untold Story of America's Concentration Camps* (Seattle: University of Washington Press, 1996), 78.

9. Esther Torii Suzuki, in *Reflections: Memoirs of Japanese American Women in Minnesota*, ed. John Nobuya Tsuchida (Covina, CA: Pacific Asia Press, 1994), 102. "In our detention center, days dragged endlessly."

10. Mary Tsukamoto, in Tateishi, *Justice for All*, 13.

11. Mine Okubo, *Citizen 13660* (Seattle: University of Washington Press, 1983), 51.

12. Gladys Ishida Stone, in Tsuchida, *Reflections*, 320.

13. Kimi Kodani Hill, *Topaz Moon: Chiura Obata's Art of the Internment* (Berkeley: Heyday Books, 2000), 3–38.

14. Chisako Joyce Hirabayashi, in Tsuchida, *Reflections*, 404. "People were trying to organize classes and projects to keep people busy and usefully occupied" (Tsukamoto, in Tateishi, *Justice for All*, 13).

15. My use of the word *loss* is informed by the scholarship of David L. Eng and David Kazanjian, *Loss: The Politics of Mourning* (Berkeley: University of California Press, 2003); and Judith Butler, *Psychic Life of Power* (Stanford: Stanford University Press, 1997).

16. Yasuko Amano, "Women Make 'Belts of 1000 Stitches' for Nisei Soldiers," *Heart Mountain Sentinel*, February 20, 1943, 8.

17. Kotono Kato, interview by Mary Tsukamoto, May 3 and 10, 1989, in Sacramento, Oral History Project of the Japanese American Citizens League (Florin chapter), and Oral History Program, California State University, Sacramento (OHP-CSUS).

18. "Buddhists Busy Making Small Scrolls," *Denson Tribune*, May 18, 1943, 3.

19. "The Boom Town Part III: A Day in the Relocation Center," YWCA Records, no. 025–18, box 50, folder 5, 50, Sophia Smith Collection, Smith College.

20. Sonoko Iwata to Shigezo Iwata, June 19, 1942, Iwata Papers, MSS 53, 2–3, Historical Society of Pennsylvania, Philadelphia.

21. Kiyoke Kodama to Mr. and Mrs. Iwata, from Poston Elementary School, January 21, 1944, MSS 53, box 2, Historical Society of Pennsylvania, Philadelphia.

22. Suzuki, in Tsuchida, *Reflections,* 94.

23. Kato, interview.

24. The 700 killed include many Japanese Americans living in Hawaii who were not imprisoned in the camp.

25. Mrs. Mitsuye Kamada, testimony before the Commission on Wartime Relocation and Internment of Civilians, New York City, November 23, 1981, reel 6, 52–53, National Archives and Records Administration; Brian Niiya, ed., *Encyclopedia of Japanese American History: An A–Z Reference from 1868 to the Present* (New York: Checkmark Books, 2001), 163–164.

26. Akiyo Deloyd, testimony before the Commission on Wartime Relocation and Internment of Civilians, Los Angeles, August 4, 1981, reel 2, 88, National Archives and Records Administration.

27. Yoshiko Uchida, *Desert Exile: The Uprooting of a Japanese-American Family* (1982; repr., Seattle: University of Washington Press, 2000), 134. See Gary Y. Okihiro, *Storied Lives: Japanese American Students during World War II* (Seattle: University of Washington Press, 1999), for more information about the National Japanese American Student Relocation Council.

28. For discussions of Wakasa's death, see Roger Daniels, *Asian America: Chinese and Japanese in the United States since 1850* (Seattle: University of Washington Press, 1988), 228–231; Sandra Taylor, *Jewel of the Desert: Japanese American Internment at Topaz* (Berkeley: University of California Press, 1993), 136–147; Okubo, *Citizen 13660,* 181; Uchida, *Desert Exile,* 140. Coverage of the incident can also be found in the *Topaz Times* between April 12 and 20, 1943.

29. "Model Plane Meet July 4," *Santa Anita Pacemaker,* June 27, 1942, 3.

30. "Model Plane Intrigues Youngsters," *Santa Anita Pacemaker,* May 26, 1942, 3.

31. "Glider Exhibition and Model Airplane Flying," *Topaz Times,* December 24, 1942, 2.

32. "Model Planes, Tins, Tubes, Gardens," *Tanforan Totalizer,* June 13, 1942, 4.

33. "Model Airplane Enthusiasts Await Wood," *Camp Harmony Newsletter,* August 1, 1942, 1.

34. "Model Plane Classes Start," *Manzanar Free Press,* June 2, 1942, 3.

35. "Aero Club Meets," *Manzanar Free Press,* June 13, 1942, 3.

36. "Model Plane Meet," *Manzanar Free Press,* July 7, 1942, 4; "Art Center Opens," *Manzanar Free Press,* June 6, 1942, 3.

37. "Rideable Plane Built in Center, *Santa Anita Pacemaker,* July 15, 1942, 3.

38. BI, "Recreation," *Tanforan Totalizer,* August 15, 1942, 9; Charles Kikuchi, *The Kikuchi Diary: Chronicle from an American Concentration Camp,* ed. John Modell (Urbana: University of Illinois Press, 1993), 224; Okubo, *Citizen 13660,* 100.

39. Mary Kobayasi, Rohwer autobiography no. 68, English 11-B, period 1, December 10, 1942, Gould/Vogel Collection, McGehee, AR.

40. "Kite Contest," *Tanforan Totalizer,* July 11, 1942, 9.

41. Allen H. Eaton, *Beauty behind Barbed Wire: The Arts of the Japanese in Our War Relocations Camps* (New York: Harper and Brothers, 1952), 86–87.

42. Girls Collect Scraps to Make Toys, Gadgets," *Santa Anita Pacemaker* June 6, 1942, 2.

43. Kiyoko Ike, Rohwer autobiography no. 66, English 11-B, period 1, Gould/Vogel Collection.

44. Betty Kanameishi, "Net Workers Make Use of Burlap," *Santa Anita Pacemaker,* June 16, 1942, 2; U.S. Army, Western Defense Command and Fourth Army, *Final Report: Japanese Evacuation from the West Coast, 1942* (Washington, DC: U.S. Government Printing Office, 1943), 205–206; U.S. Commission on Wartime Relocation and Internment of Civilians, *Personal Justice Denied,* 146.

45. "Brief History of the YWCA: Fujin Kai, Denson, Arkansas," August 2, 1943, YWCA I, box 49a, folder 4, 2, Sophia Smith Collection.

46. Mary Tsukamoto to Miss Briesemeister, Denver YWCA, May 4, 1943, YWCA I, box 49a, folder 4, 1, Sophia Smith Collection.

47. Hoshiko Keenedo to Miss Briesemeister, Rohwer, AR, June 14, 1943, YWCA Records, no. 02S-18, box 50, folder 3, 1.

48. Aiko Tanamachi Endo, interview by Marsha Bode, November 15, 1983, Nisei Experience in Orange County, CA, O.H. 1750, 30, Historical and Cultural Foundation of Orange County, Japanese American Council, and OHP-CSUF.

49. Uchida, *Desert Exile,* 61–62.

50. Yoshito Wayne Osaki, in *From Our Side of the Fence: Growing Up in America's Concentration Camps,* by Japanese Cultural and Community Center of Northern California, ed. Brian Komei Dempster (San Francisco: Kearny Street Workshop Press, 2001), 52–53.

51. *Inside View: Japanese American Evacuee Center at Rohwer, Arkansas, 1941–45* (McGehee, AR: Desha County Historical Center, 1979), 6.

52. Nobuko Hanzawa, Rohwer autobiography no. 135, English 4, period 2, December 1942, Gould/Vogel Collection.

53. Estelle Ishigo, *Lone Heart Mountain* (Los Angeles: Anderson, Ritchie, and Simon, 1972), 5.

54. Miyuki Aoyama, "Spruce Use of Wood Good: Creation Is Sensation," *Santa Anita Pacemaker,* June 27, 1942, 4.

55. Hatsuye Egami, *The Evacuation Diary of Hatsuye Egami,* ed. Claire Gorfinkel (Pasadena, CA: Intentional Productions, 1996), 78–79; and "Woodwork Class," *Manzanar Free Press,* February 3, 1943, 2.

56. Egami, *Evacuation Diary*, 78–79; and "Woodwork Class," 2.

57. Monica Sone, *Nisei Daughter* (Seattle: University of Washington Press, 2000), 181.

58. Shiro Nomura, "Inside Manzanar during World War 2," *Inyo Museums News Bulletin*, August 1975, pt. 10A, 8.

59. D.M., "He Kept Their Toes Dry!" *Camp Harmony Newsletter*, June 17, 1943, 1–2.

60. Kaoru Ito, interview by Dorothy Okura and Chisato Watanabe, December 4, 1997, Stockton, CA, Oral History Project of the Japanese Americans Citizens League and OHP-CSUS.

61. In 1920 the average annual earnings of teachers in the United States was $936, or $78 per month. Douglas Paul, *Real Wages in the United States, 1890–1926* (Boston: Houghton Mifflin, 1930), 382.

62. *Ai* translates into English as "love," and *leen* translates as "neighbor," thus the name Aileen Sewing School.

63. For plant life indigenous to southeastern Arkansas, see the Native Plant Information Network, http://www.wildflower2.org (accessed March 22, 2008).

64. Yoshie Mary Tashima, interview by Pat Tashima, February 15, 1974, Japanese American Evacuation, O.H. 1360, 4, OHP-CSUF. "We lost all of our belongings, all of out memoirs, all of our annuals. Well we lost everything" (ibid.).

65. Note from MRJ about art classes, box 9, Gould/Vogel Collection. At Rohwer, tin cans were scavenged from the mess hall trash bins and hammered into metal sculptures, and discarded buttons were used for jewelry making.

66. Michi Tashiro, "Transformation of a Rice Sack," in Japanese Cultural and Community Center of Northern California, *Our Side of the Fence*, 87–90.

CHAPTER 6 — CONTEMPORARY LEGACIES OF LOSS

1. David L. Eng and David Kazanjian, "Introduction: Mourning Remains," in *Loss: The Politics of Mourning*, ed. David L. Eng and David Kazanjian (Berkeley: University of California Press, 2003), 3.

2. According to Freud, egos mediate the conflicting functions of our ids and superegos. We are all born with ids, the part of our mind that represents our impulses. Vital for newborns, the id is intent on filling basic human needs such as satisfying hunger and avoiding pain. With no consideration for the needs of others, the id impatiently wants what feels good. By the age of three, the ego develops to mediate the needs of the id. Firmly rooted in a growing awareness of external and situational constraints, the ego makes reasoned decisions and judgment. In the context of mourning and melancholia, the ego is comprised of the residues of successfully resolved losses. The superego develops by the age

of five and is the moral part of us deciphering right from wrong. Thus the id is grounded in pleasure and the ego in reality, with the superego representing our conscience.

3. Judith Butler, "Afterword: After Loss, What Then?" in Eng and Kazanjian, *Loss*, 467.

4. Takao Shinitani, interview by Mary Tamura, 1994, Terminal Island Life History Project, Japanese American National Museum 2001, Los Angeles.

5. Jim Lobe, "Number of Anti-Muslim Incidents Jumps 30 Percent," *Inter Press Service*, September 18, 2006; and Council on American-Islamic Relations, "Executive Report," http://www.cair.com/cair2006report (accessed June 27, 2007).

6. George E. Curry, "Bush Lied about Spy Program," *New York Beacon*, May 18–24, 2006, 8; Sandy Sorensen, "Will Walls and Wire Tabs Really Keep Us Safe?" *Philadelphia Tribune*, June 6, 2006, 5A.

7. To read about the use of census records after Pearl Harbor, see William Seltzer and Margo Anderson, "After Pearl Harbor: The Proper Use of Population Data in Time of War," paper presented at the Annual Meeting of the Population Association of America, Los Angeles, March 2000; also available at the American Statistical Association's Statisticians in History Web site.

8. Lynette Clemetson, "Homeland Security Given Data on Arab Americans," *New York Times*, July 30, 2004, A14; Eric Lipton, "Panel Says Census Move on Arab Americans Recalls World War II Internments," *New York Times*, November 10, 2004, A19; Electronic Privacy Information Center, "Freedom of Information Documents on the Census: Department of Homeland Security Obtained Data on Arab American From Census Bureau," http://www.epic.org/privacy/census (accessed July 2, 2007).

9. Ambika Ahuga, "Thailand Deports 163 Ethnic Hmong Asylum-Seekers Back to Laos," Associated Press (state and local wire), June 9, 2007.

10. Sudarsan Raghavan, "War in Iraq Propelling a Massive Migration," *Washington Post*, February 4, 2007, A01; http://www.washingtonpost.com (accessed July 5, 2007).

11. Deborah Willis, "Krisitne Yuki Aono: Installing Memories," in *Fresh Talk/ Daring Gazes: Conversations on Asian American Art*, ed. Elaine Kim, Margo Machida, and Sharon Mizota (Berkeley: University of California Press, 2003), 83–85.

12. E. McClung Fleming, "Artifact Study: A Proposed Model," in *Material Culture Studies in America*, ed. Thomas Schlereth (Walnut Creek, CA: Alta Mira Press, 1999), 169.

Index

agency, 125, 163–164
Akahoshi, Seiko, 92
American Friends Service Committee, 29, 30, 50, 134
Aono, Kristine Yuki, 162
art, 1, 4, 5, 6, 14, 88, 96
artificial flowers, 5, 29–30, 107, 108; funeral wreaths, 135; paper, 4, 50, 98, 136–138
art shows. *See* exhibits
assembly centers: Anita Funita art show, 112, 138; art school, 119–120, 129; camouflage-net project, 143–144; classes, 90; Fresno, 11, 16, 53; gardens, 59–60; Handicraft Haven, 113, 120; lakes, 56–58, 79, 141; Merced, 16; Pomona, 17, 92; Puyallup, 15, 39, 80, 83, 98, 126, 139, 148; Santa Anita, 19, 21, 24, 54, 66, 90, 96, 98, 102, 111, 126, 141; Stockton, 19, 24, 126, 150; Tanforan, 12, 16, 20, 21, 24, 27, 39, 40, 56, 89, 115–116, 129; Tulare, 11, 22, 27, 45, 53, 66, 111; Versed, 16; Walegra, 35; YWCA, 142

baseball, 93–94; fields, 53, 78, 82
basketball, 78, 82
bathing facilities, 11
bon-kei, 36–37
Breed, Clara, 102
brush covering, 69
Bureau of Indian Affairs, 65

camp art shows. *See* exhibits
camp-made art, 1, 4, 5, 7, 125, 155, 164
camp newspaper: *Denson Tribune*, 107; *Heart Mountain Sentinal*, 43, 81, 118, 119; *Manzanar Free Press*, 22, 114, 122, 141; *Santa Anita Pacemaker*, 60, 113; *Tanforan Totalizer*, 20
Cato, Shuzo Chris, 25
Census Bureau, 158
ceramics, 27; densonware, 84, 107–108
classes, 3, 116–123; artificial-flower-making, 104, 121–122, 123; ceramics, 119; carpentry, 103; crotcheting, 120; flower arranging, 117, 121; ikebana, 105, 149, 150; knitting, 97, 103, 120, 150; needlecraft, 121, 123, 149; painting, 123; sketching, 123; sewing, 92, 120, 122, 150
classrooms, 43, 45–47
Colorado River Indian Reservation, 65
Commission on Wartime Relocation and Internment of Civilians, 1, 176n83
concentration camps, 1, 3, 10, 52, 128, 157, 167n2. *See also individual concentration camps*
Council on American-Islamic Relations, 157
crafts. *See* art

Darfur, 160
DeCristoforo, Violet, 16
Deloyd, Akiyo, 136

Department of Homeland Security, 158
Department of Justice facilities, 58, 76,
    95, 111, 132; Fort Missoula, Montana,
    127; Lordsburg, New Mexico, 65
Department of Justice prisons. *See*
    Department of Justice facilities
depression, 126–128
displays. *See* exhibits
Doi, John, 59

Egami, Sachi, 99
ego, 195n2
Endo, Aiko Tanamachi, 144
Executive Order 9066, 1, 5, 10, 20, 65,
    72, 103, 127, 129, 134, 138, 155, 161
exhibits, 3, 22, 101–116, 125

farm projects, 69
FBI, 22, 29, 76
Federal Bureau of Investigation. *See* FBI
Federal Bureau of Prisons, 95
flower making. *See* artificial flowers
forced leisure interpretation, 7–8
442nd Regimental Combat Team, 130
Fuhara, Kamayashi, 107
Fujikado, Toyonosuke, 148
Fujimani, Yeisaku, 115
Fujita, Jr., Henry, 139
Fukasawa, George, 26
Fukuyama, Fmuiko, 97
Furato, Yukiko, 22
furniture, 5, 24, 111; making 2, 4,
    18–21; supplies, 25–27

gardening. *See* gardens
gardens, 51, 61; community, 53, 69;
    flower, 53; fruit, 85; rock, 53, 75; veg-
    etable, 53, 85
getas, 83, 99, 111, 148
Gila (Rivers), 11, 18, 21, 25, 65, 126;
    Butte Camp section, 48, 65–66; Canal
    Camp section, 45, 65–66; YWCA, 45
golf courses, 3, 53, 78–80
Granada (Amache), 11, 12, 18, 21, 24,
    29, 41, 43, 135; impressions of, 63;
    YWCA, 45

Hanzawa, Nobuko, 20, 98
Harada, Dorothy, 94
Hashimoto, Fusaye, 18
Hatano, Masao, 105

Hatchimonji, Kumezo, 68, 69
Hayakawa, Senator Samuel Ichiye, 1, 7,
    167n1, 168n3
Hayami, Stanley, 81, 93
Hayashi, Fumi, 82, 92
Heart Mountain, 11, 27, 33, 39, 43, 44, 80,
    92, 93, 129, 135; Art Students League,
    109, 116; ceramics factory, 118–119;
    community garden, 68–70; Congress of
    American Citizens (Fair Play Commit-
    tee), 129–130; living conditions, 17–18
Hibi, Haruko, 115
Hibi, Matsusaburo, 115
Hirahara, Mrs., 32
Hmong, 159
holidays, 43; Christmas decorations,
    37, 43–44
Homma, Mrs. Mary Shigeo, 33, 117
Honma, Shigee, 105
Hosokawa, Rube, 139
hospitals, 43
hot capping, 69

ice skating rinks, 3, 53, 78, 80–82
identity formation, 51, 84, 87, 88, 153
Iida, Lillian, 76
Ike, Kiyoko, 143
ikebana, 2, 30–36, 50, 149–150
Ikeda, George, 59
Immigration Acts, 10
Internment camps. *See* concentration
    camps
Ishigo, Estelle, 142, 146
Ishino, Florence, 102
Ishino, Margaret, 102
issei, 10, 58, 89, 179n16
Ito, Grace, 123
Ito, Jimmy, 69
Ito, Kaoru, 149–150
Ito, Kimi, 109
Iwata, Masahiro, 132–134
Iwata, Shigezo, 132–134
Iwata, Sonoko, 134

Jerome (Denson), 11, 27, 36, 41, 42, 84,
    106, 115, 120; cabinet shop, 47–48;
    Fujin Kai (mother's club), 115, 144;
    gardening, 67; Young Buddhist Asso-
    ciation, 132
jewelry: bracelets, 151; lapel pins, 96,
    113, 151; rings, 5, 96; shell, 5, 151

Karen refugees, 160
Kasai, Midori, 142
Kashiwagi, Sumi, 120
Kato, Alfred, 131
Kato, Kotono, 131
Kato, Roy, 131
Kato, Shuzo Chris, 25
Katrina survivors, 160
Kawakami, Tets, 139
Kayasaki, Kamekichi, 43
Kikuchi, Charles, 20, 89
Kikuchi, Jack, 21
Kikuchi, Tom, 89
Kimura, William, 19
Kinoshita, Linda, 122
Kitamura, Ichiro, 109
Kitashima, Tsuyako, 16
kobu, 2, 35, 36, 50, 105–107, 109, 161
Kunazawa, Richard, 141
Kunitsugu, Katsumi, 92
Kuwahara, Bob, 12

landscapes: mental, 50, 164; physical, 5,
    50, 51, 164
landscaping. See gardens
latrines, 11, 12
laundry, 11–12
living units, 2, 14–50
loss, 1, 5, 54, 155–158, 168n7, 192n15; of
    business/vocation, 148–149

mailboxes, 38, 41–43
Manzanar, 11, 18, 25, 44, 99, 113, 121;
    Art Center/Art Institute, 109; chil-
    dren's village, 75–76; community gar-
    dens, 72–76; impressions of, 63–64,
    71–72; Visual Education Museum,
    113; Wing Nuts club, 141
Marumoto, Fumi, 22
material culture, 6. See also art
Matsuda, Yoshio, 21
Matsumoto, Harry, 76
Matsumoto, Ken, 112
Matsumoto, Kumiko Kariya, 81
Matsuno, Takatow, 76
Matsushita, Hanaye, 127
McCabe, Lillian, 125
melancholia, 155–156, 168n7
mess halls, 11, 43, 50, 105
Minidoka (Hunt), 11, 22, 26, 49 80, 134,
    142; furniture making, 25

model boats, 53, 57–58, 89, 141–142, 156
model planes, 113, 138–141
Monitor, The, 78
Morioka, Grace, 45
Morita, Yeneji, 109
Murao, Helen, 127
Murata, Hideo, 127

Nagumo, Reiko, 109
Nakadate, Mrs., 103
Nakagawa, Eizo, 109
Nakagawa, Kitty, 60
Nakamura, Florence Miho, 20
Nakamura, Molly, 34
Nakata, Roy, 102
nameplates, 38–43
National Security Agency, 158
needlework, 2, 50; crotcheting, 27, 29;
    embroidery, 27, 37, 50, 97, 111; knit-
    ting, 27, 90, 93, 111, 124; sewing, 27,
    29, 90, 98, 151–152; weaving, 27
Negoro, Minnie, 118
1913 Alien Land Law, 67
Ninomiya, Mrs., 26
nisei, 10
Nishi, Akira, 73
Nishimi, Shigeno, 34–36
Noda, Kasen, 117
Nomura, Shiro, 99

Obata, Chiura, 115, 119, 129
Ogura, Yumi, 122
Ohye, Henry, 138
Okamoto, Senka, 35
Okubo, Mine, 40, 96, 115, 129
Osaki, Yoshito Wayne, 145
Ota, Mable, 126–127
outdoor play equipment, 89
Owens Valley, 71
Oyama, Clem, 118
Oye, Martha Inouye, 49
Ozawa, Kenneth, 139

painting, 2
Patriot Act, 157, 158
pets, 144–148. See also wood carving:
    pets
portrait drawing, 98, 151
Poston (Colorado River), 11, 12, 21, 22,
    26, 65, 80, 93, 114, 117, 135; class-
    rooms, 46; impressions of, 18, 78;

Poston (Colorado River) *(continued)*,
 Poston I, 45, 46, 65; Poston II, 65;
 Poston III, 65, 103; YWCA, 45
privacy: lack of, 95, 99; screens, 22
psychic, emotional, mental well-being,
 4

Quakers. *See* American Friends Service
 Committee

religion: butsudan, 48; spaces of worship, 43
re-territorialization, 2, 3, 21–24, 51, 53,
 55, 60, 78, 84–87, 161, 168n4
Robertson, Guy, 117
Rohwer, 11, 21, 24, 25–27, 26, 32, 43,
 84, 89, 98, 121, 126, 142, 144; gardening, 67
Roosevelt, President Franklin Delano,
 1, 10

Sanda, Karon, 146
Sasaki, Joseph, 84, 107
Sato, Rosa, 118
Satow, Roy, 123
sculptures, 37
senninbari, 129–130
sense of place, 5, 50, 87; portable, 14,
 52, 87
sewing machines, 92, 99
Shimizu, Tsuyako, 65
Shinno, Pat, 108
Shirai, Nobori, 26, 94
skating rinks. *See* ice skating rinks
St. Joseph News Press, 78
Stone, Gladys Ishida, 129
Sugihara, Masako, 118
Sugitachi, Mary, 126, 191n1
sumo wrestling, 53, 78, 82
Supreme Court, 10
survival: emotional and physical, 1, 12,
 68; mental spaces of, 4, 12; places of
 14, 49
swimming pools, 3, 78, 80

Tahara, Kamaemon, 115
Takahashi, Moto, 81
Takahashi, S., 59
Takesako, Eidi, 115
Tamaki, Mary, 122
Tamaki, Tomae, 134
Tanaka, Mrs.

Tanamachi, Aiko, 46
Tanibata, Mas, 63–64, 78
Tashima, Yoshie Mary, 21, 63
Tashiro, Yukino, 151–152
Tateishi, Harry, 69
Taylor, Paul, 27
Tedera, Duke, 110
temporary imprisonment facilities. *See*
 assembly centers
Terminal Island, 76, 110–111, 156
Toba, Mrs., 19
Tokuda, Sakusaburo, 69
Tolan, John, 35, 176n83
Topaz, 11, 18, 21, 22, 24, 28, 29, 81, 82,
 92, 96, 121, 136–138, 139; elemen-
 tary school, 45–46; high school, 94;
 impressions of, 60–63, 181n27; living
 conditions, 16–17
Torigumi, Ben, 118
toys, 142
transnational understandings, 5, 52
Tsugawa, Hisaichi, 141
Tsukamoto, Mary, 53, 101, 121
Tsukimura, Mrs. Alice, 98
Tule Lake (Newell), 11, 22, 26, 33–35, 37,
 89, 93, 102, 121; community gardens,
 76–77

Uchida, Dwight Takushi, 23
Uchida, Iku, 124
Uchida, Yoshiko, 16–17, 145
Ueysugi, Mas, 41, 63
U. S. government, 10, 46, 52, 60

Wakasa, James Hatsuik, 136
Wakatsuki, Jeanne, 75
walkways, 2, 83–84
War Relocation Authority, 21, 25, 33, 65,
 87, 98, 116, 118, 134, 149; internal security forces, 26
Watanabe, Roy, 56, 79
West Coast exclusionary areas, 52
wood carving, 4, 111, 123; pets, 4, 146–
 147; sculptures, 37
Wood crafting. *See* wood carving

Yamamoto, Bill, 47
Yamashita, M., 139
Yanari, Kimi, 25
Young Women's Christian Association.
 See YWCA
YWCA, 45, 101

About the Author

JANE E. DUSSELIER is an assistant professor at Iowa State University with a dual appointment in the department of Anthropology and the Asian American Studies Program. Her published works include "Embodied Identity? The Life and Art of Estelle Ishigo" (*Feminist Studies*) and "Does Food Make Place? Food Protests in Japanese American Concentration Camps" (*Food and Foodways*).